BONA FIDE PURCHASE OF GOODS

T0371279

THE POSITION AND RIGHTS
OF A
BONA FIDE PURCHASER
FOR VALUE
OF GOODS IMPROPERLY OBTAINED

(BEING THE YORKE PRIZE ESSAY FOR THE YEAR 1918)

BY

J. WALTER JONES, B.A., LL.B.

OF THE INNER TEMPLE, BARRISTER-AT-LAW. FORMERLY SCHOLAR OF
EMMANUEL COLLEGE, GEORGE LONG PRIZEMAN, BARSTOW SCHOLAR

CAMBRIDGE
AT THE UNIVERSITY PRESS
1921

TO
MY MOTHER

PREFACE

THESE pages have no pretensions to be considered an exhaustive statement of the law relating to the purchase of goods. The limitation of the subject to "goods improperly obtained" has prevented any but incidental treatment of the law of factors, negotiable instruments and bills of lading, and questions of criminal law have not been explored. The American reports have been constantly drawn upon and my indebtedness to the works of Ames, Pollock and Maitland, Benjamin, Salmond and other writers is apparent on every page. One or two cases have been added whilst the essay was passing through the press. My acknowledgements are due to my brother Mr G. L. Jones, M.A. of Emmanuel College for kindly finding time to prepare the Index of Cases.

J. W. J.

25 LORD STREET,
LIVERPOOL.
Dec. 1st, 1920.

CAMBRIDGE
UNIVERSITY PRESS

University Printing House, Cambridge CB2 8BS, United Kingdom

Cambridge University Press is part of the University of Cambridge.

It furthers the University's mission by disseminating knowledge in the pursuit of education, learning and research at the highest international levels of excellence.

www.cambridge.org
Information on this title: www.cambridge.org/9781107544703

First published 1921
First paperback edition 2015

A catalogue record for this publication is available from the British Library

ISBN 978-1-107-54470-3 Paperback

Cambridge University Press has no responsibility for the persistence or accuracy of URLs for external or third-party internet websites referred to in this publication, and does not guarantee that any content on such websites is, or will remain, accurate or appropriate.

CONTENTS

PART I. INTRODUCTORY

PART II. POSITION OF PURCHASER TOWARDS OWNER

PART III. POSITION OF PURCHASER TOWARDS OTHERS THAN THE OWNER

LIST OF PRINCIPAL TEXT-BOOKS, &c., USED

ASHBURNER, *Equity*.

ATTENBOROUGH, *Recovery of Stolen Goods*.

BENJAMIN, *Sale of Goods*.

BEVEN, *Negligence*.

BLACKBURN, *Sale of Goods*.

BROWN, *Sale of Goods*.

BYLES, *Bills*.

CHALMERS, *Sale of Goods*

GIRARD, *Manuel Élémentaire de Droit Romain* (4th ed.).

Harvard Law Review (H.L.R.).

HOLDSWORTH, *History of English Law*.

HUVELIN, *Droit des Marchés*.

Law Quarterly Review (L.Q.R.).

MAYNE, *Damages*.

POLLOCK, *Contracts*.

POLLOCK AND MAITLAND, *History of English Law* (P. & M.).

POLLOCK AND WRIGHT, *Possession* (P. & W.).

SALMOND, *Torts*.

WILLIAMS, *Personal Property*.

The latest editions, except where otherwise stated.

PART I

INTRODUCTORY

CHAPTER I

THE GENERAL RULE

THE position of a bona fide purchaser of goods from a person who has improperly obtained them depends upon the answer given by the law to the problem: Which of two innocent parties is to suffer from the knavery of a third? The purchaser's merits, clearly greater than those of the vendor himself, have led common law judges to describe his position towards the true owner in terms derived from the courts of equity. Thus, according to Buller, J., in *Lickbarrow v. Mason* " he who has bought a thing for a fair and valuable consideration, and without notice of any right or claim by any other person, instead of having equity against him has equity in his favour, and if he have law and equity both with him he cannot be beat by a man who has equal equity only[1]." His position, therefore, depends entirely upon the rules of the common law and, where injustice may so often result, the only satisfactory way to solve the problem is " to apply rigorously, the settled and well known rules of the law[2]." As to these more differences of opinion are said to have arisen amongst mercantile men than amongst lawyers[3].

The policy of the Courts has been, so far as accords with justice, to promote the commerce of the nation, by making the circulation and negotiation of property "as quick, as easy, and as certain as possible[4]." This has been stated by two great judges to be the aim of the mercantile community also. "Men of business practically ascertain how much confidence may be safely bestowed, or rather whether the inconvenience and hampering of trade which is avoided by this confidence is too

---

[1] Smith, *Leading Cases* (12th ed.) Vol. I. 726, at p. 765; Pollock and Wright on Possession, p. 93.
[2] Per Lord Cairns, L.C., Cundy *v.* Lindsay (1878), 3 App. Cas. 459, at p. 463.
[3] Willes, J., Fuentes *v.* Montis, L.R. 3 C.P. 268, at p. 276.
[4] 1 Sm. L.C. 765; Scott *v.* Surman (1742) Willes, 400, per Willes, C.J. p. 407.

heavy a premium against the risk thus incurred[1]." "The object
of mercantile usages is to prevent the risk of insolvency not
of fraud; and anyone who attempts to follow and understand
the law merchant will soon find himself lost if he begins by
assuming that merchants conduct their business on the basis
of attempting to insure themselves against fraudulent dealing[2]."
It has been contended that this end is best secured by pre-
ferring the purchaser to the true owner and, accordingly, it has
been stated as the general rule that "a purchaser, for a fair
and valuable consideration, in the usual course of trade, without notice of any conflicting claim, or any suspicious circumstances to awaken inquiry or to put him on his guard, will be
protected in his purchase, and unaffected by any latent
claim[3]."

There is, however, no doubt that neither by the civil, nor
by the common law, has this ever been recognized as the
general principle. In English law, "the general rule is un-
doubted, that no one can transfer a better title than he himself
has[4]." *Nemo plus juris ad alium transferre potest quam ipse
habet.* The apparently contradictory maxim, *In aequali jure
melior est conditio possidentis*—or, as Lord Mansfield put
it[5], "Where there is equal equity, possession must prevail;
and the equity is equal between persons who have been equally
innocent and equally diligent"—has, therefore, more weight
in equity than at law; whilst possession, being possibly pre-

---

[1] Lord Blackburn, Speight *v.* Gaunt, 9 App. Cas. at p. 19.
[2] Bowen, L.J., Sanders *v.* Maclean, 11 Q.B.D. 327, 343.
[3] Jones, C.J., Saltus *v.* Everett, 20 Wend. (N.Y.) 267, at p. 276, 32 Am. Dec.
541, overruled on appeal. See also Bell, *Comm.* I. 305 (quoted in Brown, *Sale
of Goods*, p. 112 (n.)) where the general rule is said to be "that the purchaser of
moveables at market or otherwise, in bona fide, acquires the right to them, although
they have been sold by one who is not the owner."
[4] Whistler *v.* Forster (1863) L.J.C.P. 161, 164; Cundy *v.* Lindsay, *supra*; Root
v. French, 13 Wend. (N.Y.) 570, 572; Sale of Goods Act, 1893, s. 21. The Roman
rule (Dig. 50. 17. 54) was the result of the principle "Traditionibus et usucapionibus
dominia rerum, non pactis transferuntur," these modes of alienation being possible
only to the owner or his agent. (Girard, pp. 282, 294, 543.) In Germany title to
goods stolen or lost can only be given by public auction. Civil Code, arts. 935,
383. The French rule "Possession vaut titre" seems to be the result of the influence
of Germanic customs upon the Roman rule. Goods lost or stolen may be recovered
in three years, except in a few cases where the price must first be repaid; these, however, are wider than the exceptions in our law. French Civil Code, arts. 2279, 2280.
As to the Canadian Code see 5 App. Cas. 664.
[5] Ancher *v.* Bank of England, 2 Doug. 637, at p. 639.

carious, criminal, or qualified is, though evidence, only *prima facie* evidence, of title[1].

Even when the goods are sold by a person intrusted with them by the owner, the general tendency of the Courts has always been to restrict facilities of misapplication; and they have inclined still more strongly to prevent the unlawful disposition of goods by persons who have improperly obtained them. The rare exceptions to the rule are based upon principles introduced into the common law, either by the usages of merchants, or by the application of equitable principles where the scale of diligence can be turned against the true owner. Moreover, the judges have considered that, in this way, they have promoted, rather than discouraged, the transaction of commercial operations ; and it has been said that such legislation as the Factors' Acts giving exceptional protection to innocent purchasers, " has been, generally speaking, a greater favourite with the city than with the profession[2]."

Purchasers and pledgees have constantly argued that business would be hampered if they had to inquire into the possessor's authority. Lord Bramwell has dealt with this argument with his usual force. In *Colonial Bank v. Cady*[3] he said : " The same thing was said when Lord Sheffield's Case[4] was decided. But, as has been shrewdly observed, such business is as lively as ever....Shopkeepers have said, when suing a husband, that they could not possibly ask the wife if she had his authority to pledge his credit—she would be offended. An excellent reason for not asking her—but not for making him pay." Business men must be content,—as Lord Blackburn, in words already quoted, said they are,—to take the risk. " There are risks which men engaged in business must be content to encounter, and against which the law can afford them no protection. The law can punish roguery, but it cannot secure innocent persons against losses from its multi-form devices[5]." The rule has been said to serve the interests of

[1] See per Lord Loughborough, Mason v. Lickbarrow, 1 Sm. L.C. p. 744.
[2] Lord Brougham, Wilson v. Moore, 1 My. & K. 337, 358. Cf. per Best, C.J., Williams v. Barton 3 Bing. 139, p. 145.
[3] 15 App. Cas. 267, p. 282.　　　　[4] 13 App. Cas. 333.
[5] Burton v. Curyea, 40 Ill. 320 ; 89 Am. Dec. 359.

commerce in states where there is a large foreign and domestic
trade "by protecting the property of the stranger, as well as
of our own citizens, against the possible frauds of carriers by
sea, or by internal transportation, whilst it throws upon the
resident merchant the responsibility of taking care with whom
he deals, and teaches him a lesson of wholesome caution[1]."

The Factors' Acts have done much to promote commerce,
but it is doubtful whether they can go much further without
increasing the insecurity they were enacted to prevent; moreover, the same considerations do not apply where the goods
have been improperly obtained, even by factors. Cases are
bound to arise, from time to time, bringing up the question in
an acute form. It is not long since the House of Lords, by
emphasizing the general principle that a man's property
cannot be divested without his own consent, prevented an
extension of the common law going far beyond the Factors'
Act in the protection of innocent purchasers[2].

When the bona fide purchaser is described as the "favourite
of modern law[3]," it is, therefore, statute law to which reference
is made, for the Courts have shown little disposition to limit
the rights of the owner. Nevertheless, owing to the peculiarly
technical rules of the older common law, it frequently occurred
that a purchaser from a wrongful possessor could keep the
goods in peace. Since the decay of the old appeal of larceny,
the owner of goods tortiously taken has never had an action
which assured him their return in specie, and even at the present
day, he can only rely upon the discretionary power of the
Court. The wrongful taker, therefore, "gained by his tort both
the possession and the right of possession; in a word, the
absolute property in the chattel[4]"; and the idea that the
trespasser acquired the property prevented an action of trespass for any subsequent dealing with it, even by another
person[5]. That trespass does not lie against a purchaser from

---

[1] Verplanck, Senator, in Saltus v. Everett, 20 Wend. (N.Y.) 267, p. 283,
32 Am. Dec. 541.
[2] Farquharson v. King (1902), A.C. 325.   [3] P. & M. II. 154.
[4] Ames, Select Essays in Anglo-American Legal History, III. p. 549.
[5] Ames, ib.; Bro. Abr. Tresp. 358, quoting Y.B. 21 Ed. IV. 74. Though Fitz-
herbert (Abr. Avow. 151) says a thief acquired the property, an appeal could be
brought against a second taker Y.B. 4 H. VII. 5, 1; P. & M. II. 164. As to purchase from bailee Y.B. 2 Ed. III. 5, 9; 21 H. VII. 39, 49; Bro. Abr. Tresp. 216, 295.

a tortious taker is still good law, but it is the received opinion that until the rise of detinue *sur trover* in the fifteenth century, superseded later by the modern action of trover and conversion, no action of any kind lay against the purchaser[1]. The defendant was protected, whether innocent or dishonest, for the requirement of good faith and absence of notice, which is sometimes added in this connection, can only be described as a "characteristically modern qualification[2]." The rule was, in fact, not the result of modern principles in favour of free trade, but of the technicalities of the old forms of action.

Prof. Ames has shewn that at equity, in the same way, the purchaser in good faith of land subject to uses, though always protected, was not specially favoured, for, until the middle of the fifteenth century, the cases where the use was enforced against third parties were the exception rather than the rule[3]. When, gradually, equitable and legal rights were enforced against purchasers, the Courts of equity, owing to their peculiar procedure *in personam* which enabled them to probe men's consciences, found it possible to draw the line at purchasers in good faith, whilst the common law courts, except where the sale was in market overt according to rules which helped to ensure good faith, had to give an action against any purchaser, honest or not[4].

The difference between the principles of law and equity was clearly seen in the not infrequent case of an owner who, having a good claim at common law for the recovery of his goods from a bona fide purchaser, came to equity in order to have assistance to enable him to discover which of the goods were in the defendant's hands. In courts of equity the plea of a purchase for value without notice was

---

[1] Ames, *ib.* p. 554; Holdsworth, H.E.L. III. 276, 277, who thinks the work of detinue *sur trover* was formerly done by detinue upon a *devenerunt ad manus*; P. & M. II. 153–164.
[2] Holmes, *Common Law*, p. 169, referring to 2 Wms. Saund. 47 n. (1); the owner is barred even now when the pledge is by a bailee not at will, unless the pledge determines the bailment, Fenn *v.* Bittleston, 7 Ex. 152.
[3] Y.B. 22 Ed. IV. 6; the Chancellor said it was usual to give a subpœna against the feoffee's heir, but Hussey, C.J. (K.B.) said that 30 years before such a subpœna would not have been issued.
[4] Ames, *loc. cit.* 435, 436. See *Select Cases in Chancery* (S.S.), case 125 as to applications to the Chancellor in cases of purchases from pirates.

"an absolute, unqualified, unanswerable defence, and an unanswerable plea to the jurisdiction of the Court[1]"; and it was regarded as a cardinal principle that from such a purchaser the Court would take away nothing which he had honestly acquired[2]. Thus in some early cases, where goods were purchased from a bankrupt after his bankruptcy, it was held that the owner could obtain no relief against the purchaser[3]. In *Hoare v. Parker*[4] where a person entitled to the use of plate for her life pawned some of it to an innocent party, the plea of bona fide purchase was held good against a bill for discovery of the particular articles pawned, filed in order to proceed at law for their recovery, Lord Thurlow stating that a purchaser "was not bound in conscience to assist the right owner in the legal recovery of the subjects, purchased under such circumstances." Had the Court possessed jurisdiction over the relief such a plea would have been powerless against discovery[5], for a plea which was not good against relief was equally ineffective against discovery. Since the Judicature Acts the Courts of law and equity have concurrent jurisdiction and, therefore, an innocent purchaser cannot now resist discovery[6].

[1] Pilcher v. Rawlins, 7 Ch. App. 259 per James, L.J., at p. 269.
[2] Heath v. Crealock 10 Ch. App. 22, at p. 33.
[3] Perratt v. Ballard (1681) 2 Cas. Ch. 72 where Lord Nottingham said: "It is an infallible rule, that a purchaser for valuable consideration shall never *without notice* discover anything to hurt himself." Abery v. Williams (1681) 1 Vern. 27.
[4] (1785) 1 Cox. 224; 1 Bro. C.C. 578.
[5] Williams v. Lambe (1791), 3 Bro. C.C. 264; Collins v. Archer (1830), 1 Russ. & M. 284.
[6] Ind, Coope and Co. v. Emmerson, 12 App. Cas. 300; Manners v. New, 29 Ch. D. 725; Ashburner, *Equity*, p. 70.

CHAPTER II

GOODS

"GOODS" are defined by the Sale of Goods Act, 1893 (s. 62), to exclude money and things in action, and to include emblements, and things attached to or forming part of the land which are agreed to be severed before sale or under the contract of sale. The coins of which money consists are in substance chattels, but money differs from "goods" as being an exception to the general rule that a man who has no title can give none. There is also the material distinction arising from its use as a medium of exchange, that one man's money cannot, in general, be distinguished from another's. The fact that "property in money cannot be known[1]" led to the opinion that, except when in a bag or chest, it could not be the subject of trover. Though this was not followed[2], it still remained the law that detinue could not be brought, since the judgment, being entered for the thing itself, and only, if it could not be recovered, for damages, required the identification of the specific articles[3].

The rule that an innocent taker acquired a good title was, therefore, said to be based on the peculiar difficulty of identifying money. Thus Lord Holt put it on the ground that "money or cash is not to be distinguished" and thought that lottery tickets, the subject of the action, were recoverable, since "they have distinct marks or numbers on them[4]"; and Willes, C.J., said in a later case: "For why are goods considered still as the owner's? Because they remain in specie, and so may be distinguished from the rest of the bankrupt's estate. But as money has no earmark it cannot be followed[5]."

[1] Y.B. 22 Ed. IV. 19; Bro. Abr. *Prop.* 34; Viner, Abr. *Restit.* 1.
[2] Higgs (or Hicks) *v.* Holiday, Cro. Eliz. 638, 661, 746; Draycot *v.* Piot, ib. 819; Hall *v.* Dean, ib. 841; Kinaston *v.* Moor, Cro. Car. 89.
[3] Noy, 12.
[4] Ford *v.* Hopkins (1700) 1 Salk. 284.
[5] Scott *v.* Surman (1742) Willes, 400; Whitecomb *v.* Jacob (1711) Salk. 60.

The maxim that "money has no earmark" considered as a basis for the exceptional treatment of money clearly went too far, for it would have protected takers in bad faith. This was seen by Lord Mansfield, who said of money in the hands of such persons that "it is in the nature of specific property, so that if its identity can be traced and ascertained the party has a right to recover[1]." He, therefore, as in the old cases relating to trover, considered the question of identity one of fact to be left to the jury. The old dicta were finally overthrown by Lord Ellenborough in *Taylor v. Plumer*[2] where the law was thus explained: "The difficulty which arises in such a case is a difficulty of fact, and not of law, and the dictum that money has no earmark must be understood in the same way, *i.e.* as predicated only of an undivided and indistinguishable mass of current money." Money in a bag or a coin marked for the purpose of being distinguished, he thought, was so far "earmarked" in the hands of a taker in bad faith as to be in the same position as other personal property[3].

The true ground for the exception which money forms to the general rule had, therefore, to be sought elsewhere and had already been explained by Lord Mansfield in *Miller v. Race*[4]. "It has been quaintly said: 'that the reason why money cannot be followed is, because it has no earmark': but this is not true. The true reason is, upon account of the currency of it...but before money has passed into currency an action may be brought for the money itself." Thus money is differentiated from substances like corn, which are equally hard to identify, because of "the characteristic peculiarity of money...that it is the highest degree of currency[5]." When coins have passed into currency they cannot be recovered from innocent takers for value, even when identifiable. If a man's sovereigns or shillings

---

[1] Clarke *v.* Shee (1774) Cowp. 197.
[2] (1815) 3 M. & S. 562.
[3] Cf. the Roman rule: Si alieni nummi inscio vel invito domino soluti sunt, manent eius cuius fuerint: Si mixti essent ita ut discerni non possent eius fieri qui accepit scriptum est, ita ut actio domino cum eo, qui dedisset, furti competeret. Dig. 46. 3. 78. The Courts of equity by the doctrine of a charge on a fund have extended the means of ascertainment. In re Hallett's Estate 13 Ch. D. 677, where the cases are discussed; Ex p. Cooke 4 Ch. D. 123. See an Australian Case, Black *v.* Freedman 12 C.L.R. 105.
[4] (1758) 1 Burr. 452.
[5] Wilde, B., Foster *v.* Green (1862), 7 H. & N. 881, 887.

have a private mark on them by which they can be distinguished this does not enable him to recover them from such a holder[1]. On the other hand, where a bona fide purchaser buys from a thief a £5 gold piece, by statute part of the current coin of the realm, as a curiosity, it is treated as a chattel and not as money, and can be recovered from him, for it has not yet passed into currency[2].

"Things in action," also excluded from the definition of "goods" are things in the eye of the law, *i.e.* "which are not visible or tangible or capable of manual delivery or of actual enjoyment in possession in its ordinary sense, and which, if denied, can be enforced only by action or suit[3]." Their dissimilar nature, apart from the fact that they were not directly transferable at the common law, is sufficient to prevent the application to them of the essentially common law rules relating to the sale of goods. Nevertheless, the documents by which they are evidenced are goods and the obligations thus testified to can only be transferred subject to defects of title. The influence of the law merchant upon the common law not only rendered some *choses in action* transferable but also attached to them the characteristic of negotiability—the result being that in the hands of a bona fide purchaser "the contract is completely embodied for all practical purposes in the instrument which is the symbol of the contract: and both the right under the contract and the property in the instrument are treated in a manner quite at variance with the general principles of contract and ownership[4]." That the "symbol" remains a chattel is shewn by the fact that trover lies for it; and though Lord Mansfield seems to have thought that the title to the paper, and that to the right evidenced by it, could never be in separate persons, his reason—that the paper was valueless—would not apply where, as was suggested to him, the obligation was engraved on a valuable metal, *i.e.* where there was something more than a mere symbol[5].

---

[1] Wookey *v.* Pole, 4 B. & Ald. 1.
[2] Moss *v.* Hancock (1899) 2 Q.B. 110.
[3] Colonial Bank *v.* Whinney 11 App. Cas. 426, per Lord Fitzgerald, at p. 446.
[4] Pollock, *Contracts* (8th ed.) p. 241.
[5] Perreira *v.* Jopp, note to 10 B. & C. 452; Cochran *v.* Fox Chase Bank (1904) 103 Am. St. Rep. 976. See an article by Mr Z. Chafee, Jr, H.L.R. XXXI. p. 1109.

In the case of "negotiable paper," to use an American term, we therefore find "goods" which are an exception to the general rule; and as the contract must be for the payment of money[1], it is clear that the negotiability of such paper is a result of the currency of money. The possession and property are inseparable in the hands of innocent holders "by reason of the course of trade[2]" because these instruments are "constantly and universally, both at home and abroad, treated as money, as cash, and paid and received as cash; and it is necessary for the purposes of commerce, that their currency should be established as secured[3]."

When a disseisor is in possession of land, a purchaser from him may, in some cases, acquire a good title to things of which he is wrongfully in possession, because of their connection with the freehold. Things connected with the freehold are "goods," under the above definition, either because they are emblements, *i.e.* "such vegetable products as are the annual results of agricultural labour[4]," or because they are severed or agreed to be severed at the time of the sale. Thus there are two classes to be considered:

1. (*a*) Emblements which are the results of the disseisor's labour; and (*b*) things which are not goods at the time of eviction but become so under the sale.

2. (*a*) Emblements which are the results of the disseisee's labour before eviction; and (*b*) things which, though physically attached to the soil, are not legally "fixtures[5]." These are the "goods" of the disseisee at the time of his eviction.

The disseisee's only remedy for the first class is an action for mesne profits, by which he may recover damages for loss of use and occupation of the land and also for any injury done to the land[6]. This action may be added to the claim for the

[1] Dixon v. Bovill, 3 Macq. 1.
[2] Anon. 1 Salk. 126.
[3] Lord Mansfield, Miller v. Race, 1 Burr. 452, 459; Collins v. Martin 1 Bos. & Pul. 648, 651.
[4] Williams, *Personal Property* (17th ed.) p. 150.
[5] See Hornish v. Symonds 110 L.T. 1016; Davis v. Jones 2 B. & Ald. 165; Hobson v. Gorringe (1897) 1 Ch. 182; Lee v. Gaskell 1876 1 Q.B.D. 700.
[6] The action is one of trespass. See 11 Co. Rep. 51a; Salmond, *Torts*, c. 6.

recovery of the land, but cannot be brought against a purchaser of the goods who is not in possession of the land, and who therefore acquires a good title to the goods[1], though he may be aware of the rival claim.

Though it seems that the owner might bring trover for the second class against the purchaser, the action for mesne profits against the disseisor in possession would here, also, be the most convenient course, for the plaintiff must prove his title to the land in order to recover them[2].

[1] Any other rule would give the real owner the gross produce irrespective of the expense of production, which, where there is a claim of right, would be unjust. See the American cases Johnston v. Fish 105 Cal. 420, 45 Am. Rep. 53 ; Page v. Fowler, 39 Cal. 412 (crops); Brothers v. Hurdle 10 Ired. 490, 51 Am. Dec. 400 (trees). In these cases there was a claim of right to the land and in the first the purchaser knew of the rival claim.

[2] See later, p. 75, for the case of goods which become part of the freehold.

CHAPTER III

WHO IS A BONA FIDE PURCHASER FOR VALUE?

(i) GOOD FAITH
(ii) PURCHASE FOR VALUE
(iii) BURDEN OF PROOF

(i) GOOD FAITH.

Until the recognition by the common law courts of the doctrine that a sale in market overt passes the property, the purchaser's state of mind did not affect his title, or want of title, to the goods. So long as the appeal of larceny was still in use and the requirement of an *animus furandi* not clearly set out, the mere possession of another's goods, especially when supported by the conviction of the seller, threw upon the purchaser the suspicion of crime; and though he might, by proof of the purchase, repel this charge, he had no right to the goods[1]. It has been seen that after the decay of the appeal the technicalities of the common law often enabled him to keep goods in peace, but here, again, his rights did not depend upon his mental state. It was probably always part of the rule of market overt that knowledge of the seller's defective title prevents the passing of the property; but an early case in which the purchaser's conduct is used to prove, not that he bought in bad faith, but that he did not buy in the market at all, seems to shew that, in most cases, fulfilment of the conditions established by custom in the market was sufficient proof of absence of knowledge[2]. In the Year Books at a later period absence of knowledge still seems to sum up the good faith required; but that a rigid adherence to the usage of the market was no longer sufficient proof, is shewn by the allusions in Court to the common case of

---

[1] Britton, c. 16, 5.
[2] The Court Baron (S.S.), p. 64 : "And if thou did'st buy them with thy money in the fair of C., whither come merchants with divers merchandises from divers countries to buy and sell as thou hast said, why did'st thou hide them so secretly for so long a time?"

a wrong-doer who carries his ill-gotten wares to a market at the first opportunity, and sells them to an accomplice willing to play the part of a purchaser[1]. Mere knowledge of a defective title is distinguished in theory, though not in legal effect, from a "covinous" bargain of this kind[2].

"Good faith" began to be more fully discussed, as something different from mere absence of knowledge, when negotiable instruments became common, and when we remember that "the thought of man is not triable[3]," it is not surprising to find the Courts considering whether something less than knowledge might not be enough to deprive a purchaser of the goods.

During the eighteenth century, juries were directed to find for the bearer of a note if he acquired it bona fide, and, as a test of bona fides, Lord Mansfield was accustomed to ask them to consider whether it had been taken "fairly" or "in the usual course of business[4]." The practice of leaving to the jury the question of good faith alone was stated by Lord Kenyon in *Lawson v. Weston*[5] in 1801 to be firmly settled; any other usage, he said, would paralyze the circulation of all the negotiable instruments in the country.

Nevertheless, in *Gill v. Cubitt*[6] in 1824, a direction to find for the defendant, the acceptor, if the plaintiff had taken the bill in circumstances which ought to have excited the suspicion of a prudent and careful man, was held a proper one. Abbott, C.J., thought the case of *Lawson v. Weston* doubtful; Bayley, J., said that though the usual question had been whether the bill had been taken bona fide, "it was part of that bona fides whether the plaintiff had asked all those questions which, in the ordinary and proper manner in which trade is conducted, a party ought to ask"; and Holroyd, J., thought that the question whether it had been taken bona fide "involves in it the question whether it had been taken with due caution."

---

[1] Y.B. 33 H. VI. 5.
[2] Bro. Abr. *Tresp.* 26 "par cest covin le propertie nest alter et eadem lex si lachator conust que le vendor eux prist sans title." Also Harvey v. Facey, 2 And. 109, 115; Co. 2 Inst. II. 713.
[3] Brian, C.J., Y.B. 17 Ed. IV. 1.
[4] Miller v. Race, 1 Burr. 452; Grant v. Vaughan, 3 Burr. 1516.
[5] 4 Esp. 56, 57. See also Egan v. Threlfall (1823) 5 D. & R. 326 (n).
[6] 3 B. & C. 466; 5 D. & R. 324.

This decision was followed, during the next ten years, in a series of cases[1] of which *Slater v. West*[2] is the strongest instance. There, a person came to the defendants' warehouse and, saying he was recommended to buy from them by a person named who occasionally dealt with them, bought goods to a considerable amount and made a part payment in cash. The defendants inquired as to the persons named in the bill and were satisfied. Yet they were unsuccessful in an application for a new trial, on the ground that they had not used due caution in taking the bill. Thus, although on the facts *Gill v. Cubitt* may have been correctly decided, it was clear that, by the direction there approved and now followed, the law had been entirely changed[3]. The dicta of the judges in that case, it is true, seemed to treat caution merely as a test of good faith, but Lord Mansfield's practice[4], though professedly followed, was in fact disregarded, and diligence, not good faith, had become the test for the acquisition of a good title.

In 1834, owing, it is said[5], to the discredit into which Bank of England bills were falling and the complaints of the commercial community, the question again came before the now remodelled King's Bench. Patteson, J.[6], thought the cases had gone too far, and in the next year Parke, B., threw doubt upon *Gill v. Cubitt* as a departure of doubtful wisdom from the old law[7]. Finally, in *Goodman v. Harvey*[8] the old rule that good faith was the only question for the jury was completely restored by Lord Denman.

These cases related to negotiable instruments but the same principles were held to apply to chattels, the doctrine of *Gill v. Cubitt* having been accepted as the general rule of the common law until *Goodman v. Harvey*. Thus in *Dyer v. Pearson*[9], where the right to chattels was in question, Lord Tenterden,

---

[1] Down v. Halling (1825) 4 B. & C. 330; Beckwith v. Corrall (1826) 3 Bing. 444; Snow v. Peacock, ib. 406; Lang v. Smyth (1831) 7 Bing. 284; Wilson v. Moore (1834) 1 My. & K. 337.
[2] (1828) Dan. & Lloyd, 15.   [3] Cf. per Parke, B., 5 Tyr. p. 262.
[4] See however 2 Cowp. 479, where he required diligence; also 4 T.R. 28, where the same is true of Lord Kenyon.
[5] Phelan v. Moss, 67 Pa. St. Rep. 59, 63.
[6] Crook v. Jadis, 5 B. & Ad. 909, 910; Backhouse v. Harrison, ib. 1098, 1105.
[7] Foster v. Pearson, 5 Tyr. p. 262.   [8] (1836) 4 Ad. & E. 870.
[9] 3 B. & C. 38. A new trial was ordered for misdirection on another point.

in accordance with his opinion in *Gill v. Cubitt*, told the jury
"that if a man takes upon himself to purchase from another
under circumstances which ought to have excited his suspicion
and induced him to distrust the authority of the person selling"
he could not hold the property if it afterwards turned out that
the seller had no authority; and, under a statute setting aside
purchases from a bankrupt just before his bankruptcy unless
made bona fide, he held that a purchase, though not fraudulent,
was invalid if not in the ordinary course of trade[1].

The Sale of Goods Act, 1893, s. 62 (2), following the Bills
of Exchange Act, 1882, s. 90, enacts that "a thing is deemed
to be done in 'good faith' within the meaning of the Act when
it is in fact done honestly, whether it be done negligently or
not." That the older view is not dead is shewn by the Larceny
Act, 1916[2], which allows restitution of a negotiable instrument
in the hands of a bona fide holder unless it is taken "without
any reasonable cause to suspect that the same had been stolen,"
and by the Indian Penal Code[3] and the Indian Contract Act[4].

It was often urged that the question of due diligence was
too difficult to be left to a jury. Best, C.J., thought it was not
too extensive or too difficult for a jury of merchants or a special
jury[5], but Patteson, J., in *Crook v. Jadis* said he himself could
never understand the test, and when left to a common jury it
was stated to lead "to much perplexity and frequent injustice[6]."
The view of Lord Kenyon that it would impede commerce was
also pressed upon the judges who thought diligence necessary.
The answer, in most cases, was that it could only be to the
advantage of the commercial classes to check dishonesty which
would be encouraged by any other rule, and that "no correct
dealer can complain that he is only required to exercise such
a degree of caution as strict honesty suggests and the safety

---

[1] Ward *v.* Clarke, Moo. & M. 497.
[2] 6 & 7 Geo. V. c. 50 s. 45 (2a) re-enacting 24 & 25 Vict. c. 96 s. 100.
[3] S. 52. "Nothing is said to be done or believed in good faith which is done
or believed without care or attention, *i.e.* care and attention of a man of ordinary
prudence."
[4] S. 108. "Provided that the buyer acts in good faith, and under circumstances
which are not such as to raise a reasonable presumption that the person in possession...has no right to sell the goods."
[5] Snow *v.* Peacock, 3 Bing. 406.
[6] Phelan *v.* Moss 67 Pa. St. Rep. 59 at p. 63, quoting Chitty on Bills (9th ed.).

of others requires[1]." Where the purchaser has a suspicion that
things are not right, these considerations have great weight,
but where he is perfectly innocent they only tend to embarrass,
by unnecessary inquiries, transactions which usually have to be
carried through quickly[2].

The distinction drawn in some cases[3] between "ordinary"
and "gross" negligence was also disposed of in *Goodman v.
Harvey*. It was considered in that case that "gross negligence
may be evidence of mala fides, but is not the same thing," and
that if the jury is satisfied as to the purchaser's good faith the
presence of negligence, however exceptional, is insufficient to
affect his title. Even if, contrary to the trend of modern opinion[4],
we recognize different degrees of negligence, it is hardly correct
to say that one or two mutually exclusive states of mind can
be evidence of the other[5]. What is meant is that the facts shew
that the mental state was not negligence at all but mala fides,
as may indeed be inferred from the use by some judges of the
expression "gross or *wilful* negligence," a term otherwise in-
explicable[6]. A purchaser was said to be "grossly" negligent
when he was considered to have bought the goods in circumstances which must have convinced him that they were wrongly
obtained[7], but as has often been pointed out, circumstances
which must have convinced one man may not affect another[8].

But though a purchaser does not by negligence cease to be
in good faith, the very use of the latter term shews that something more than mere absence of knowledge is required. A
purchaser who has no knowledge of a defective title is often

[1] Wilson v. Moore, 1 My. & K. 337.
[2] Willis, *Negotiable Securities* (3rd ed.), p. 17.
[3] *E.g.* Backhouse v. Harrison, 5 B. & Ad. 1098.
[4] Hinton v. Dibbin, 2 Q.B. N.S. 661; Wilson v. Brett, 11 M. & W. 113; cf.
Giblin v. McMullen, 2 P.C. 337 and Beven, *Negligence* (2nd ed.), p. 1624.
[5] Salmond, *Jurisprudence*, s. 143; Ashburner, *Equity*, p. 87.
[6] *E.g.* Turner, V.-C., Hewitt v. Loosemore, 9 Hare, 449, 458, James, L.J.,
Ratcliffe v. Barnard, 6 Ch. App. 652, according to whom it is only another name
for such facts as the jury may consider evidence of knowledge of a fraud.
[7] Sheppard v. Shoolbred, Car. & M. 61.
[8] The Roman definition seems to agree in rejecting any external standard.
See D. 50. 16. 108 (Modestinus): "Bonae fidei emptor esse videtur, qui ignoravit
eam rem alienam esse, aut putavit eum qui vendidit ius vendendi habere." Cf.
Erskine's *Institutes of Law of Scotland*, Bk. 2, c. 25, where a purchaser is said to
be mala fide if "he may on the slightest reflection know that he (seller) is not the
rightful owner," and Ramsay v. Wilson (1665), Mor. 9114. By German Civil Code,
Art. 932, gross negligence is equivalent to bad faith.

said to have "notice" of it. The word "notice" in this connection is as old as the Year Books where it seems to mean nothing more than knowledge[1]. The equity Courts in dealing with trusts used the word in a much wider sense where, on the facts, the ignorance of the purchaser was beyond dispute. Lord Hardwicke based the equitable doctrine upon fraud or mala fides and to this extent there is no doubt that it is recognized by the common law also, though the term has not, at least until the last century, been much used in the common law Courts. The Sale of Goods Act, 1893, requires the absence of notice as well as the presence of good faith[2].

If the ground of the doctrine of notice "is the fraud or mala fides of the party, then it is all one, whether by the party himself or his agent[3]," and it is established that this rule is part of the common law also, being based on principles of liability which pervade all its branches. The agent must be acting for his principal's benefit and it must be his duty to communicate the facts to him[4]. The same principle applies to joint purchasers, one of whom is in bad faith. In *Oppenheimer v. Frazer and Wyatt*[5] a person who had wrongly obtained goods handed them to *B* to sell for him. *B*, who acted in bad faith, sold them to a friend who purchased in good faith and agreed with *B* that the purchase should be on the joint account of *B* and himself. He debited *B* with half the purchase price and having sold at a profit credited him with half the gain. Although he had come in as a purchaser after the goods had come into *B*'s hands, he was held not to be in good faith. "Where two persons so purchase as joint-purchasers, it cannot be said that the persons taking under the disposition act in good faith..., if either of them acts in bad faith[6]."

This "imputed notice" is sometimes called, in Courts of

---

[1] *E.g.* Y.B. 9 H. VI. 45; Harvey *v.* Facey, 2 And. 115.
[2] Ss. 22 (1), 23.
[3] Le Neve *v.* Le Neve, Amb. 436, 447, 1 Ves. 64, 68; Willoughby *v.* Willoughby, 1 T.R. 763, 767.
[4] Irving *v.* Motley, 7 Bing. 543; Kettlewell *v.* Watson, 21 Ch.D. 685. It was held in Dresser *v.* Norwood (1864) 17 C.B. (N.S.) 465, that a purchaser was bound by knowledge acquired by his agent in a prior transaction. But see now the Conveyancing Act, 1882 (s. 3), which applies to personal as well as to real property, s. 1 (4).
[5] 1907 2 K.B. 50 (reversing 1907 1 K.B. 519).
[6] Fletcher Moulton, L.J., *ib.* at p. 68.

equity, "constructive notice[1]," a term usually, however, applied
to cases where there is no vicarious bad faith. In working out
the rules relating to trust estates the Courts of equity held that
a purchaser might be bound by facts which would have been
brought to his notice if he had made the usual investigations
into title[2], and the equitable doctrine, which has here clearly
departed from its original basis of bad faith, is for this reason
inapplicable to goods. As Lord Erskine said in *Hiern v. Mill*[3]:
" There is a marked distinction in this respect between a real
estate and a personal chattel. The latter is held by possession,
a real estate by title." Consequently the common law Courts
have frowned upon any attempt to introduce this doctrine into
commercial transactions. In *London and Joint Stock Bank v.
Simmons*[4], Lord Herschell said he would be very sorry to see
the doctrine introduced into the law of negotiable instruments
and in *The Manchester Trust v. Furness*[5] Lindley, L.J., expressed the same view in these words: "In dealing with estates
in land title is everything, and it can be leisurely investigated;
in commercial transactions possession is everything, and there
is no time to investigate title; and if we were to extend the
doctrine of constructive notice to commercial transactions we
should be doing infinite mischief and penalizing the trade of
the country." These considerations apply with as much weight
to chattels as to negotiable instruments. Even in equity the
doctrine is not likely to be extended[6]. In *Joseph v. Lyons* it
was thought to have been carried too far and to be inapplicable
even to chattels whose title could be investigated in registers
of bills of sale[7].

The result is that the purchaser is not put upon inquiry as
to any defect of title where he has no suspicion that anything
is wrong[8]; when he has such suspicion, on the other hand, he

[1] Hiern v. Mill, 13 Ves. 114 per Erskine, L.C., p. 120; Kettlewell v. Watson,
21 Ch.D. per Fry, L.J., p. 704.
[2] See Ashburner, *Equity*, p. 86 *et seq.*   [3] *Ubi sup.*   [4] (1892) A.C. 221.
[5] (1895) 2 Q.B. 545; cf. Dawson v. Prince, 2 De G. & J. 50, per Turner, L.J.
[6] Ware v. Lord Egmont, 4 De G.M. & G. 460.   [7] 15 Q.B.D. 280.
[8] The statement that commercial law does not recognize "constructive" notice
must be received cautiously in one case for "it has been held that actual authority
that the person dealing (with the purchaser) is an agent with a limited authority,
puts the other upon inquiry as to the extent of his title," 2 Wh. & Tu. 223; Cooke
v. Eshelby (1887), 12 App. Cas. 271. This is in any case inapplicable to cases of
improper obtaining.

is not necessarily deprived of protection, for his failure to make inquiries may be due to negligence, which, however gross, will not affect his position. Suspicion must continue to be nothing more than suspicion, and the best proof of this is that the purchaser made a fair inquiry, and received an answer which he believed to be true and which he is, therefore, entitled to act upon[1]; not that he is bound to make such inquiry, but, having done so, he is clearly acting in good faith. For suspicion may become something more. Instead of negligently paying no heed to suspicious circumstances the purchaser may turn his back upon them and resolve not to see anything contrary to what he conceives to be his interests. In such a case he is liable under the rules both of law and of equity for he is acting in bad faith, and good faith is the same in the law merchant, as introduced into the common law, as in equity[2].

The distinction between negligence and wilful abstinence from inquiry was carefully explained in *Jones v. Smith*[3] by Wigram, V.-C. After speaking of cases "in which the Court has been satisfied from the evidence before it that the party charged had designedly abstained from inquiry for the very purpose of avoiding notice" (which he classes as an instance of "constructive" notice, notice here being clearly equivalent to knowledge) he goes on to say that the proposition of law upon which they proceed "is not that the party charged had incautiously neglected to make inquiries, but that he had designedly abstained from such inquiries for the purpose of avoiding knowledge—a purpose which, if proved, would certainly shew that he had a suspicion of the truth, and a fraudulent determination not to learn it." In *Jones v. Gordon*[4], Lord Blackburn adopted the rule as part of the common law in words which are as applicable to chattels as to bills or notes. "If a man knowing that a bill was in the hands of a person who had no right to it, should happen to think that perhaps the man had stolen it when if he had known the real truth, he would have found, not that the man had stolen it, but that he had obtained it by false pretences, I think

---

[1] Macbryde v. Eykyn (1871), 24 L.T. 464.
[2] Ames, *Cases on Bills*, p. 714; also 1 Hare 43 per Wigram, V.-C., at p. 71.
[3] 1 Hare 43, 55; also per Fry, L.J., In re Morgan, 18 Ch.D. 93, 102.
[4] 2 App. Cas. 616, 628.

it would not make any difference, if he knew that there was something wrong about it and took it. If he takes it in that way he takes it at his peril." Here also negligence was differentiated and the ignorance was described as "wilful if not simulated." Again, in a case where the seller had been guilty of a fraud Byles, J., said: "It is not necessary that the party should know all the circumstances of it. If he suspected a fraud and chose not to ask, lest he should know, he had sufficient notice[1]." Thus, though means of knowledge[2] are not enough in themselves, they are treated as actual knowledge where the purchaser fraudulently makes no use of the opportunities they offer of discovering the truth. " Notice and knowledge mean not merely express notice, but knowledge or the means of knowledge to which the party wilfully shuts his eyes[3]," so that the common law has no need to resort to the equitable doctrine of "constructive notice" in order to cover this well-recognized class of cases, which are clearly based on fraud or "wilfulness." It has been suggested[4] that the term "general or implicit notice" might be advantageously opposed to "that particular or explicit notice" which is in reality better called knowledge; it would express the position of a purchaser who has knowledge that there is *some* illegality or *some* fraud vitiating the title, though he may not have been apprised of its precise nature.

The use of the word "notice" in the Sale of Goods Act, in addition to good faith must, therefore, be understood to mean the "imputed notice" resulting from agency or joint purchase, the conception of good faith being sufficient to cover all the other recognized cases where a purchaser is deprived of the protection he would otherwise have at common law.

It may be well to give some instances of the application of the above principles to the sale of goods by one who has no title.

---

[1] Oakeley v. Ooddeen, 2 F. & F. 656, 659; see also London and Joint Stock Bank v. Simmons, 1892, A.C. 221.

[2] "That is a very vague expression, and it is difficult to say with precision what it amounts to; for example, it may be that the party may have the means of knowledge on a particular subject, only be sending to, and obtaining information from, a correspondent abroad." Kelly v. Solari, 9 M. & W. 54.

[3] May v. Chapman, 16 M. & W. 361.

[4] Byles on Bills (17th ed.) p. 144. In a case in *Select Pleas in the Court of Admiralty* (S.S. Vol. VI.) 141, 236 (t. H. VIII.) we find a plaintiff alleging (1) notice, or (2) a strong conjecture and suspicion, (3) gross negligence.

As it is often a difficult matter to trace the history of particular goods, one of the chief ways of proving mala fides is by shewing that the purchaser was so well aware of the vendor's embarrassed circumstances, that he took the risk that the articles had been obtained without any intention to pay for them or by other fraudulent means. Thus in a case under an old Bankruptcy Act[1], the bankrupts, "endeavouring to make a purse" for themselves, bought more goods than usual, just before the bankruptcy, and their agent told the defendants that the goods were to be sold at a sacrifice and made statements from which the defendants knew that the sellers were in difficulties. He also told them that the transaction was to be kept private and when he refused to name the sellers they said: "Just shove us in the name of a seller" upon which the witness gave his own. The jury found, and were held warranted in finding, on these facts, that the purchasers did not act in good faith, but wilfully shut their eyes to the facts[2]. The same result occurred where a pawnbroker bought the stock of a trader in a hasty manner, without making inquiries as to his indebtedness or why he wanted to sell in a hurry, and where in addition he did not call the vendor as a witness[3]. On the other hand, in the case of a purchase from a fraudulent vendee with a voidable title, it is not enough to shew that it was generally known in the neighbourhood that he was a common mercantile swindler[4].

It seems that a distinction should also be made between a sale and a pledge for a sum considerably less than the value of the goods, for a man is more likely, when in embarrassed circumstances, to borrow on the security of his own goods than to sell them at a sacrifice. Lord Mansfield in 1760 dealt with this very case in these words: "A notion that lending money to traders knowing them to be in dubious, tottering or distressed circumstances, upon mortgages or liens is fraudulent...would throw all mercantile dealing into inextricable confusion. Men lend their money to traders upon mortgages or consignments

[1] 6 Geo. IV. c. 16 s. 82.
[2] Devas v. Venables, 3 Bing. N.C. 400.
[3] Hare v. Saloon Omnibus Co., 4 Drew 492.
[4] Cleveland Woollen Mills v. Sibert, 81 Ala. 140.

of goods, because they suspect their circumstances and will not run the risk of their general credit[1]." In a more recent Scottish case, where *A* induced a sale by fraudulent statements as to his solvency, and then pledged the goods with *B*, these dicta were cited with approval[2]. The Court went further, and it was said to be "an abnormal and unheard of proposition that, before you buy or take an article in pledge, you must satisfy yourself not only that the article is the property of the seller or pledgor, but that he has accounted to the person from whom he may have got the article." However, though good faith is, in both cases, necessary and sufficient, a jury would probably be harder to satisfy where there was a sale than where there was merely a pledge; but it must be satisfied as to the purchaser's mental attitude to the fraud not merely to the insolvency.

Thus, especially where there are other circumstances, inadequacy of consideration is a fact upon which practical men will place great reliance[3], but, in itself, it is not decisive. "If a person goes to a shop, and seeks to buy goods as cheap as possible, how does he become a party to a fraud because he gives a small price for the goods[4]?" In the same way, payment of the full value is not conclusive proof of good faith, although it would be very strong evidence indeed of the honesty of the transaction where the purchaser is dead or cannot be called as a witness[5].

Knowledge of embarrassed circumstances and inadequacy of consideration are only two out of very many facts which may influence the jury. Since direct proof is very rarely, if ever, possible, "the credibility of the witnesses, their interest in the case, the reasonableness or unreasonableness of their statements, the time, place, and manner of the transaction, its conformity to, or its departure from, the ordinary method of business[6]" and many other matters all help to produce an effect. The Court only decides whether there is sufficient evidence to

[1] Foxcroft *v.* Satterthwaite, 2 Burr. 931, 942.
[2] Price *v.* Bank of Scotland, 1910, S.C. 1095, 1110, 1118, per Lord Dunedin.
[3] Miller *v.* Race, 1 Burr. 452; Price *v.* Neal, 3 Burr. 1355; Jones *v.* Gordon, 2 App. Cas. 616, where £1727 worth of bills were sold for £200.
[4] Lee *v.* Hart, 10 Ex. 555 per Platt, B. at p. 560.
[5] See Lord Esher's opinion quoted in Byles on Bills (17th ed.) p. 144.
[6] Winter *v.* Nobbs, Ann. Cas. 1912 C. 19.

go to the jury, or on appeal, whether the verdict is perverse or unreasonable[1]; it is the jury which decides the honesty of the transaction, and since its verdict will be carried into effect, " it furnishes the means to make men honest, even against their wills, and although there may not be much virtue in legal honesty, there is a good deal of utility in it[2]."

(ii) PURCHASE FOR VALUE.

The rules of the common law relating to the rights of a purchaser of goods from a wrongful obtainer are, in general, equally applicable to a mortgagee, who is a purchaser *pro tanto*[3], and to a pledgee[4], and their assignees. Execution creditors are not classed as purchasers[5], even when they buy at an execution sale[6]; nor are trustees in bankruptcy[7].

More important is the question:—What is valuable consideration? The Sale of Goods Act, 1893[8], applies only to transactions for "a money consideration, called the price," but the principles of the common law, relating to the title to goods, on which the corresponding sections of the Act are based, apply to purchasers for any valuable consideration. "Valuable," contrasted with "good" or "meritorious" consideration which is that of natural love and affection[9], may consist "either in some right, interest, profit or benefit accruing to the one party, or some forbearance, detriment, loss, or responsibility given, suffered or undertaken by the other[10]." "There is no question... that the consideration of marriage is the highest known to the law[11]."

---

[1] Fletcher Moulton, L.J., Oppenheimer *v.* Frazer and Wyatt, 1907, 2 K.B. 50, 68; Solomons *v.* Bank of England, 13 East 135 (n).
[2] Farr *v.* Sims, 24 Am. Dec. 396, Rich. Eq. Cas. 122.
[3] Lord Hardwicke, Willoughby *v.* Willoughby, 1 T.R. 763, 767.
[4] Cf. the position of pledgees under the rules of market overt, and their liability in conversion (*infra*). Kennedy, L.J. (1911, 1 K.B. 487), doubted whether s. 23 of the Sale of Goods Act applied to a pledgee, but thought he was protected at common law.
[5] Burgh *v.* Burgh, Rep. t. Finch 28; Brace *v.* Marlborough, 2 P. Wms. 491.
[6] Farrant *v.* Thompson, 5 B. and Ald. 826. Devoe *v.* Brandt, 53 N.Y. 466; Sargent *v.* Sturm, 23 Cal. 359.
[7] In re Eastgate (1905), 1 K.B. 465; Tilley *v.* Bowman (1910), 1 K.B. 745; the "reputed ownership" clause does not apply to goods improperly obtained, 4 & 5 Geo. V. c. 90 s. 38 (2c).   [8] S. 1 (1).
[9] "Good" sometimes means "valuable," *e.g.* Copis *v.* Middleton, 2 Madd. 410, 430; Wigan *v.* English &c. Association 1909, 1 Ch. 291, 302.
[10] Currie *v.* Misa, L.R. 10 Ex. 153, 162.   [11] Ford *v.* Stuart, 15 Beav. 493, 499.

The consideration most likely to raise difficulties in the ordinary dealings of trade is that of an antecedent debt. According to the definition in *Currie v. Misa* it is no consideration for a simple contract, the general rule being that "an antecedent debt is not, in itself, a sufficient consideration for anything beyond the implied promise to pay it[1]." The Courts have gone far to imply some detriment on the creditor's part, so that such a debt is valuable consideration where there is pressure on his part[2], forbearance promised[3], or even actual forbearance at the debtor's request though not for any specified time[4]. It has recently been said that the cases where the existence of such a debt has been held not a sufficient consideration for a voluntary increase of a security "are cases where that voluntary increase of the security was not known to the creditor and, therefore, could not possibly have influenced him in the way of forbearance[5]."

By an extension of the notion of forbearance it is possible that the original owner may himself be held a purchaser for value of goods formerly taken from him and returned. Thus, in one case, securities which were stolen from the defendants by their manager and came into the possession of the plaintiffs, bona fide purchasers for value, were subsequently obtained back from the plaintiffs by the manager by fraud, and restored to the defendants, who were unaware that they had left their possession. It was held that, in the absence of contrary proof, it should be presumed that the defendants accepted the securities in discharge of their manager's obligation to return them, and were, therefore, holders for value[6]. The decision was based on the ground that the manager, though guilty of crime, was also liable for conversion of the securities and "when he restored them they lost their right, for how could they bring an action for the conversion of instruments which were in their own

---

[1] Crofts *v.* Fenge, 4 Ir.Ch.R. 316, 317; Vaughan Williams, L.J., Glegg *v.* Bromley, 1912, 3 K.B. 474. It is assumed that the debt is a valid one, not a gaming debt. See Kenny, *Criminal Law*, p. 225.

[2] Cracknell *v.* Janson, 11 Ch.D. 1.

[3] Miles *v.* N. Z. Alford &c. Co., 32 Ch.D. 266.

[4] Alliance Bank *v.* Broom, 2 Dr. & Sim. 289; Wigan *v.* English &c. Association 1909, 1 Ch. 291 where the cases are reviewed.

[5] Fletcher Moulton, L.J., in Glegg *v.* Bromley *ubi sup.*

[6] London and County Bank *v.* London and River Plate Bank, 21 Q.B.D. 535.

possession" (Lord Esher, M.R.) and that "a man may fairly be presumed to assent to that to which he in all probability would assent if the opportunity of assenting were given him" (Lindley, L.J.). However, a plaintiff may recover damages for loss due to a conversion, even after the goods are back in his hands; and the implied consideration was described as "somewhat artificial" in a later case where it was remarked: "If someone steals my boots, and afterwards replaces them, one might perhaps—but not, I think, without some strain on the imagination—conceive that I impliedly release my right to complain of the theft, in return for the restored boots, though I did not know them to have been stolen[1]." Such circumstances, though not probable in connection with goods, are possible. *A* steals goods from *B* and sells them to *C* in market overt; he subsequently re-obtains them from *C* under a contract induced by fraud and returns them to *B*'s possession, the latter being ignorant of the theft.

Though a pre-existing debt is not, in itself, sufficient to support a simple contract, it was held in *Currie v. Misa* that it was enough to constitute the creditor a holder for value of a bill[2], and this is the law under the Bills of Exchange Act 1882[3]. Again, in *Taylor v. Blakelock*[4] Bowen, L.J., said: "By the common law of this country the payment of an existing debt is a payment for valuable consideration. Commercial transactions are based upon that very idea." In *Leask v. Scott*[5] it was decided that it was sufficient to defeat the unpaid owner's right of stoppage *in transitu* and Bramwell, L.J., said there was no trace of a distinction to be found in the books between cases of past and present consideration. This was a case of a bill of lading, which is, in this respect, akin to a negotiable instrument, but he added that there was no authority to shew that a past value is not sufficient in the analogous

---

[1] Nash *v.* De Freville (1900), 2 Q.B. 72 per Collins, L.J., p. 88.
[2] The bill was payable on demand so that the fiction of forbearance did not apply.
[3] S. 27. It is distinctly differentiated from a consideration sufficient to support a simple contract.
[4] 32 Ch.D. 560, 570.
[5] (1877) 2 Q.B.D, 376; Rodger *v.* Comptoir d'Escompte &c. L.R. 2 P.C. 393 dissented from; cf. Chartered Bank of India *v.* Henderson, L.R. 5 P.C. 501 where there was pressure.

case of goods obtained under a fraudulent contract where the vendor loses his title on a transfer for value[1]. Thus the same rule seems to apply to goods as to negotiable instruments. The ground for protecting the purchaser being that he has altered his position to his detriment, it might be argued that this cannot apply to a past debt ; on the other hand, it might be said that such a creditor is lulled into security. " He rests on the belief that his debt is paid, and in that belief foregoes all effort to seek other payment[2]." Moreover, such a past consideration has always a present operation, for it stays the hand of the creditor, and to apply a different rule to goods and to negotiable instruments would be to introduce needless niceties into commercial law[3].

The American cases are in conflict, but the weight of authority is said to be in support of the view, that unless the purchaser parts with a new consideration, surrenders some security or evidence of indebtedness, or in some other way changes his legal status to his detriment, he is not a purchaser for value of goods[4]. Story, J., thought that the same principles did not apply to negotiable instruments as to goods[5]; and it has been said that the distinction is a necessary one, growing out of the difference in character or quality of the thing transferred in its relation to commerce[6].

A further distinction is drawn in some states between a transfer in payment of a pre-existing debt and as security for such debt. There is the same conflict on the question whether a purchaser of chattels who pays partly in cash and partly by the extinguishment of a pre-existing debt is a purchaser for value, but the preponderating opinion seems to be in his favour. Where the cash payment is relatively very small and only provided in order to give a semblance of a valuable consideration, different principles come into play[7].

---

[1] p. 382.   [2] Butters v. Haughwort, 42 Ill. 18, 89 Am. Dec. 401.
[3] Bramwell, L.J., in Leask v. Scott *ubi sup.*
[4] See note to Ann. Cas. 1918 A. p. 455.
[5] Moore v. Godfrey, 3 Story, 364, cited by Ames, *Cases on Bills*, 1. p. 650, who thinks the different rules strangely inconsistent.
[6] Ames Iron Works v. Kalamazoo &c. Co., 63 Ark. 92.
[7] Victoria Paper Mills Co. v. New York &c. Co., Ann. Cas. 1918 A. p. 455. The precautions seem to imply bad faith.

Provided the Court is convinced of the reality of the consideration, it will not weigh it in "golden scales[1]," because "in purchases the question is not whether the consideration be adequate, but whether it be valuable[2]." In such a case the only effect of inadequacy, both at law and in equity, is to raise a presumption of mala fides where the inadequacy is gross and there are other questionable circumstances[3]. But the Court may think the consideration (e.g. five shillings) merely colourable and nominal, on the ground not of inadequacy, but that the transaction is not a sale at all, being in fact a gift concealed under the outward semblance of a sale.

The old cases on the rule of market overt allege actual payment of the specified sum on the spot[4]. If we may draw an analogy from the cases relating to land, absence of bad faith must continue until the payment of the whole sum, so that a purchaser who becomes aware of the fraud after part payment of the price cannot claim a lien for the amount paid, but there seems to be no authority on the point[5]. Otherwise, if there is good faith at the time of payment subsequent knowledge does not affect the purchaser's position. *Mala fides superveniens non nocet*[6].

(iii) BURDEN OF PROOF.

It is not necessary for the owner of goods to prove the exact way in which they left his hands, for in many cases, *e.g.* where a watch is stolen from a private drawer or a horse taken from a field, it is obviously impossible[7]. After proof that they were in the owner's possession the purchaser is left to make out his claim to them. This corresponds with the conceptions upon which trover is founded, the older form alleging merely a "*devenerunt ad manus.*"

In the case of bills of exchange there seems to have been

[1] Mathews v. Feaver, 1 Cox, 278, 280; "diamond scales," Roe v. Mitton, 2 Wils. 358 (n).
[2] Basset v. Nosworthy, Rep. t. Finch 102.
[3] Copis v. Middleton, 2 Madd. 410, 427; Pollock, *Contracts* (8th ed.), p. 657. In sales by auction the price is generally presumed to be adequate, Aldborough (Earl of) v. Trye, 7 Cl. & F. 436.
[4] Y.B. 12 Ed. IV. 8, "prae manibus solut."
[5] See Doswell v. Buchanan's Exors., 13 Leigh 365, 23 Am. Dec. 280.
[6] See for the rules of Roman Law, Girard (4th ed.), p. 304 (n).
[7] Down v. Halling, 4 B. & C. 330, per Abbott, C.J., p. 334.

some doubt whether, upon proof of fraud or illegality in the
acceptance or issue, the holder had to prove good faith in
addition to value; eventually it was settled that he had to
prove both[1], and this is the rule laid down by the Bills of
Exchange Act 1882[2]. So also in the case of *In re Nisbet and
Pott's Contract*[3], Farwell, J., said: "The plea of purchase for
value without notice is a single plea, to be proved by the
person pleading it. It is not to. be regarded as a plea of purchaser for value, to be met by a reply of notice." When the
owner has proved his loss it consequently lies upon the purchaser, in the rare cases where he can acquire a title from a
wrongful obtainer to prove good faith and value.

But it was held in *Whitehorn Bros. v. Davison*[4] that where
the purchaser had bought from a person with a voidable title
the onus lay on the plaintiff, on the ground that since the
property is in the purchaser by virtue of a title, though a
voidable one, it must be displaced by the defrauded seller.
Again, in the case of a sale in market overt, it is difficult to
see what evidence can be clearer proof of good faith than the
purchase itself according to the usages of the market, so that
here also in practice the burden would fall upon the owner to
prove specific bad faith[5].

---

[1] Bailey *v.* Bidwell, 13 M. & W. 73; Smith *v.* Braine, 16 Q.B. 244; Jones *v.*
Gordon, 2 App. Cas. 616, 627, 628; Tatam *v.* Haslar, 23 Q.B.D. 345.

[2] S. 30 (2).

[3] (1905) 1 Ch. 391, 402 approving Att. Gen. *v.* Biphosphated Guano Co., 11
Ch.D. 327, 337.

[4] (1911) 1 K.B. 463; for the rule when the seller is an agent or factor see per
Kennedy, L.J. and Buckley, L.J. referring to Oppenheimer *v.* Frazer and Wyatt
(1907), 2 K.B. 50. In America in most jurisdictions the purchaser must prove both,
though good faith is *prima facie* made out by proof of sale in the ordinary course
of business (38 Am. St. Rep. 504).

[5] See also Burkinshaw *v.* Nicholls, 3 App. Cas. 1004, 1017, 1018 per Lord
Cairns as to burden of proof in cases of estoppel. In the early cases the allegation
of bad faith was generally made in answer to the plea of purchase in market overt
according to the custom of the market. Y.B. 33, H. VI. 5 (1), 12 Ed. IV. 8.
Where the purchase is open and fair though not in market overt, Lord Hardwicke
thought the plaintiff should be required to prove his case "in the strictest manner."
Haris *v.* Shaw, Cas. t. Hard. 349.

PART II

POSITION OF PURCHASER TOWARDS OWNER

CHAPTER IV

ACQUISITION OF OWNERSHIP

A PURCHASER from a wrongful obtainer, as we have seen, in general acquires no title; indeed, as he may be liable for conversion his title may often be "worse than none." The general rule applies even though the sale be by a sheriff under a *fi. fa.*[1] The exceptions are

    (i) where the sale is market overt;

    (ii) where the owner is precluded from asserting his title;

    (iii) where the improper obtaining is such as to confer on the seller a voidable title;

    (iv) where the sale confers a good title according to the law of a foreign country in which it takes place;

    (v) where there is an alteration in the nature of the goods;

    (vi) where there is a satisfied judgment for the detention or conversion of the goods;

    (vii) where the owner waives the tort[2].

Whilst good faith is essential in the first three cases, and usual in the fourth (but the question here depends on foreign law), the title is often acquired in the last three ways, which, however, have more theoretical than practical importance, by the wrongful vendor before the sale or by a mala fide purchaser.

(i) PURCHASE IN MARKET OVERT

According to Blackstone[3], it is the general rule of law "that all sales and contracts of anything vendible, in fairs or markets overt (that is, open) shall not only be good between the parties,

---

[1] Farrant *v.* Thompson, 5 B. & A. 826; Crane *v.* Ormerod (1903), 2 K.B. 37.
[2] A sale of captured goods by order of a prize court of the captor established in a neutral country does not change the title to the property. The Flad Oyen 1 C. Rob. Adm. 134. The English law contains no provision such as exception (2) in the Indian Contract Act, s. 108 relating to sales by one of several joint-owners, which, however, only applies where one has possession with the consent of the others.
[3] *Comm.* II. p. 449.

but also be binding upon all those that have any right"; a rule codified in the Sale of Goods Act, 1893, thus: "where goods are sold in market overt, according to the usage of the market, the buyer acquires a good title to the goods, provided he buys them in good faith and without notice of any defect or want of title on the part of the seller[1]."

As the doctrine of market overt is often described as part of a peculiarly Saxon institution it is worth while giving some attention to the rules existing on the subject in England before the Conquest. A person found in possession of property recently in the possession of another was presumed to have stolen it; but one method of rebutting the charge was by proof of his purchase, and if the seller refused to warrant the title, it might be proved by witnesses, before whom all sales had to be transacted[2]. Proof of purchase did not entitle him to keep the goods, but by the early laws of Hlothaere and Eadric[3], a purchaser in London, on disproving the charge of theft by a witness testifying to an open sale, could claim the value of the chattel. This exceptional provision does not seem to have been preserved in later legislation and falls short of the modern rule, but it bears witness to the early commercial importance of London[4]. The later laws repeatedly forbid sales of goods above a certain price except before witnesses, and attempts were made, though not very successfully, to forbid all bargains except in towns[5].

After the Conquest the law remained substantially the same; ownership is never acquired from a wrongful possessor, but proof of a purchase is sufficient to acquit the purchaser of crime. In Bracton[6], this proof is most easily made when the purchase has been publicly transacted in a fair or market in the presence of the bailiffs or other witnesses, accompanied by the payment of toll; but the goods must be restored and

---

[1] S. 22 (1).
[2] Ine c. 25; Liebermann, *Gesetze der Angelsachsen*, I. p. 100; P. & M. II. p. 157; Holdsworth, H.E.L. II. p. 99.
[3] (*Circ.* 680 A.D.) c. 16; Liebermann, *op. cit.* p. 11.
[4] P. & M. II. p. 157; cf. Holdsworth, H.E.L. II. p. 99 who refers to the rule as a "curious anticipation of the later rule of market overt."
[5] Aethelstan II. c. 12; IV. c. 2; Liebermann, *op. cit.* 156, 171; Laws of William the Conqueror, III. 10, 11; Liebermann, *ib.* 491. In Wales fines were levied on individuals for buying and selling out of the market. See "Commote account of the proceedings at the Great Turn, 15th and 16th Ed. II." quoted Att.-Gen. *v.* Reveley, Exch. 868–9 (rep. Karslake) at p. 51.   [6] f. 151.

repayment of the price cannot be demanded. Britton[1], Fleta[2], and the Mirror[3] lay down the law in the same way. It is clear, therefore, that at the end of the thirteenth century the common law knew no rule of market overt, the only effect of a purchase in a market being to render unnecessary a warrantor, as was the case with any other purchase before witnesses[4]. The doctrine must therefore have been introduced into the common law between that date and 1430, in which year we find the rule stated in argument as well-established law[5].

We are told of the merchants frequenting the German fairs in the middle of the ninth century that "they contend that the purchase which is made at an annual fair should be valid, whether it be just or unjust, because it is their custom[6]." Later there arose in the South of France a custom, according to which the'purchaser in a fair or market, on the fixed day, could refuse to restore the goods except upon payment of the price. In this case the privilege was not, at first, due to any idea in favour of the circulation of property, but was the result of the general protection given to thieves and other malefactors who entered the lord's franchise; and of the desire of the lords to attract trade, and consequently revenue by tolls, to their estates[7]. But these reasons fell into the background as the merchants came to realize the importance of safeguarding their dealings with strangers coming from afar; and, in time, any public sale received the same protection, the requirement of good faith being brought in to keep the custom within bounds[8].

The customs which made up the Law Merchant were peculiar to no country and were therefore followed in England

---

[1] C. 16 s. 5.   [2] Bk. I. c. 38 s. 7.   [3] Bk. III. c. 13 (S.S.) p. 98.
[4] Cf. *Ancient Laws of Wales*, I. p. 681 : "Whoever shall buy anything in a market is not to have a warranty." Gwentian Code, Bk. I. c. 37 (14). See also Huvelin, *Droit des Marchés*, p. 459 (citing Du Cange, *Gloss.* "feria dicitur; haberi loco auctoris"), "Celui-là seul qui achète dans le marché achète au grand jour et est dispensé d'appeler son auteur en garantie."
[5] Y.B. 9 H. VI. 45 per Paston.
[6] See Royal Commission on Markets and Fairs, 1888, Vol. I. Introduction, p. 4, quoting Notker, Boethius; Scrutton, J., Clayton v. Le Roy, 1911, 2 K.B. 1031, 1039.
[7] Huvelin, *op. cit.* p. 455, quoting a Text of 1075 A.D.; *Borough Customs* (S.S.), II. pp. 47, 185, 186.
[8] See Jobbé-Duval, *Revendication des Meubles*, p. 148 *sq.*, Huvelin, *op. cit.* p. 459 *sq.*, Brissaud, *History of French Private Law*, II. p. 1201 *sq.*, for the history of the French rule contained in Art. 2280 of the French Civil Code.

as well as on the continent; but as the disputes, which were
settled in accordance with them, were decided summarily in
the Courts of the fairs and markets, it is not surprising that the
common law courts are silent on the subject of market overt
until the fifteenth century. The gradual introduction of the
modern rule can be traced in the various borough customs, for
though in those outlying parts of Scotland and Ireland where
cattle theft was common, a bona fide purchaser who could not
claim the privilege of a burgess was not even acquitted of
crime, on the other hand, in commercial boroughs, where the
influence of foreign merchants was greater, the purchaser could
claim the return of the purchase money, and in one instance
(Carrickfergus) he acquired the complete ownership. In England as early as 1181 a purchaser in Chester could claim the
price he paid from a Welsh owner; and during the next two
centuries such a claim against the owner is recognized in many
other boroughs[1]. In the roll of cases decided at the Fair of
St Ives in 1291, not only is the plea of purchase in open market
used as in Bracton's day to rebut a charge of carrying off goods,
but we find a defendant, on swearing that malt was brought
to her house by a stranger to whom she innocently lent 8d.
upon it as security, allowed to keep the goods[2]. This is clearly
a complete departure from the rule of the common law at
that time and a step beyond the customs of the merchants
in some other parts. The modern rule is early recognized in
the manorial courts[3], and finally in the reign of Henry VI is
part of the common law[4].

From the earliest times we find many cases which turn
upon the payment of tolls to the owner of the franchise and
this shews that, as on the continent, freedom of commerce
was not the only consideration which favoured the mercantile
custom. Bracton, Britton and Fleta[5] treat the payment of toll
by the purchaser as necessary to protect him from the punish-

---

[1] For the growth of borough customs see Bateson, *Borough Customs*, II. (S.S.),
LXXVI *sq.*
[2] *Select Cases in Law Merchant* (S.S.), pp. 37, 48. In another case in 1332 (p. 111)
the plea of purchase "in pleno mercatu" is again put forward as giving a title.
[3] *Select Cases in Court Baron* (S.S.), p. 64.
[4] Y.B. 9 H. VI. 45.
[5] See references above, pp. 34, 35.

ment for theft, probably on the ground that it was evidence of publicity of the sale and the absence of collusion. The Mirror says that toll was ordained "as evidence of the contract, for every privy contract was forbidden[1]." When it became the rule that a sale in market overt passed the property it was at first laid down that payment of toll was a necessary condition[2]. In the *Prior of Lanthony's Case* the Court thought that *prima facie* a plea was good which did not allege it[3], but this may have been based on the fact that the franchise in the city of London belonged to no one. In the later case of *Comyns v. Bower*[4], however, such an allegation was deemed unnecessary in the case of a market elsewhere than in London, and it is now well established that tolls are not necessarily incident to a market or fair but owe their origin to a subordinate franchise appurtenant to the fair or market[5]; and it is equally well settled by a series of cases that, where toll is due, it is payable by the purchaser and not by the vendor unless there is a custom or prescription to the contrary[6].

The decisions on tolls are useful in defining the circumstances in which a transaction can be said to be a sale in market overt; but the first and most important question is: What can be said to be a market overt? "Market" may mean

(i) A franchise conferring a right to hold a concourse of buyers and sellers[7].

(ii) The concourse itself.

(iii) The place where the concourse usually meets[8].

---

[1] Bk. I. c. 3 (S.S.) p. 14; Black. *Comm.* II. p. 449.
[2] The Crown Jewels Case, Y.B. 35 H. VI. f. 25, per Prisot and Fortesque, C. JJ. (f. 29), the former of whom said that the issue was always taken on the payment of toll. Bro. Abr. *Prop.* 9.
[3] Y.B. 2 Ed. IV. 8, pl. 22; Bro. Abr. *Tresp.* 328.
[4] Cro. Eliz. 485; Co. Inst. II. p. 713.
[5] The Maidenhead Case (1619), Palmer 76, 86, followed in Duke of Newcastle v. Worksop U.D.C. (1902), 2 Ch. 145. See per Farwell, L.J., p. 156.
[6] Y.B. 9 H. VI. 45; Orbuston v. James, Lut. 1377; also Leight v. Pym, *ib.* 1329; Bedford v. Emmett, 3 B. & Ald. 366; Att. Gen. v. Horner (2), 1913, 2 Ch. 140, and cf. 35 H. VI. 25.
[7] Cruise, Digest, *Market* (A); Marquis of Downshire v. O'Brien (1887), 19 L.R. Ir. 380.
[8] Com. Dig. *Market* (A), "the usual place where a market is held is the market, not every place within the same town."

In the expression "sale in market overt," it means the concourse. "A market, viewed in its strictly legal aspect, may be
defined as an authorised public concourse of buyers and sellers
of commodities meeting at a place, more or less defined, at an
appointed time[1]." But the peculiar rule in the City of London
tends to throw the emphasis on the place of meeting, instead
of the meeting itself; moreover, an actual gathering or crowd
is not necessary.

Fairs are usually classed with markets, and it has been said
that "every fair is a market—and not è contra—and therefore
when any statute speaks of a fair, a market should also be
comprehended[2]." It has recently been held, however, that there
is no impossibility in holding a fair and a market in the same
manor on the same day, and there is no presumption that the
market is absorbed in the fair, "the two franchises are separate
and distinct, and of equal dignity, there is no question about
a greater or less estate, such as is essential to merger[3]." For
the purpose of the sale of goods at any rate, a fair may be
described as a "great sort of market"; the only distinction being
that a market is usually held once or twice a week, a fair once
or twice a year.

The market must be a legally constituted one[4] and it has
been held that a market cannot be a legal market without a
grant (actual or presumed)[5]. In *Moyce v. Newington*[6] it was
thought that a market newly established under a recent Act
by the Corporation of Maidstone would not protect a purchaser
therein; but it has been held[7] in Ireland that the protection
given to a sale in market overt is not confined to ancient
markets created by Charter or prescription, but extends to
modern markets established under powers conferred by Act of
Parliament, *e.g.* a cattle market established by the Corporation
of Dublin under the provisions of the Dublin Improvement
Act, 1849.

---

[1] Royal Commission on Markets and Fairs, 1890.
[2] Com. Dig. *Market* (B); Coke 2 Inst. 221.
[3] Duke of Newcastle *v.* Worksop U.D.C. 1902, 2 Ch. 145 per Farwell, J., p. 155.
[4] Lee *v.* Bayes, 18 C.B. 599 per Jervis, C.J., p. 601.
[5] Benjamin *v.* Andrews, 5 C.B. (N.S.) 299.   [6] (1878) 4 Q.B. 32, 34.
[7] Ganley *v.* Ledwidge, Ir. Rep. 10 C.L. 33; approved in Delaney *v.* Wallis,
14 L.R. Ir. 31.

According to Blackstone[1] "market overt in the country is only held on the special days provided for particular towns by charter or prescription" and "the market place, or spot of ground set apart by custom for the sale of particular goods, is also in the country the only market overt." It is essential that the sale should be transacted in open market ("in pleno mercatu"), and though in the earlier cases this is based upon the lord's right to supervise the kind and quality of the goods sold and to collect the tolls due[2], it is clear that any other rule would provide an obvious instrument for giving a good title to goods wrongly obtained.

The mercantile custom as introduced in the fourteenth or fifteenth century was itself modified by the immemorial custom of London, whereby every shop in the city[3] in which goods are exposed publicly for sale is a market overt, for such things only as the owner professes to deal in; every day being a market day, except Sunday and holidays. "This is almost the only instance of a city strong enough to assert and maintain the privilege that a shop within its boundaries is equivalent to a market overt, though more than one city has attempted to assert it[4]." Thus in the "daylight purchase[5]" in Chester in the twelfth century we perhaps see a former custom of the same kind; but an attempt to establish that each shop in Bristol is a market overt was unsuccessful, on the ground that a sale in a shop did not satisfy the condition that it should be "in pleno mercatu[6]." The origin of the custom seems to be due to the fact that in early times London was commercially one large market, almost every sale, wholesale or retail, being conducted in open markets in the city, into the legal status of which the private retail shops, which succeeded them, naturally

---

[1] *Comm.* II. p. 449. [2] *E.g.* Prior of Dunstable's Case, Y.B. 11 H. VI. 19, 25.
[3] The custom applies only to the city, and is inapplicable to the Strand; Anon. 12 Mod. 521; Haris *v.* Shaw, Cas. t. Hard. 349. In Wilkinson *v.* King, 2 Camp. 335 it seems to have been thought applicable to Southwark which is outside the city, but the case went on another point. On the whole question of market overt in the City of London see a valuable article by Mr J. G. Pease, L.Q.R. XXXI. p. 270.
[4] Fletcher Moulton, L.J., Clayton *v.* Le Roy (1911), 2 K.B. 1031, 1047. In the Prior of Dunstable's Case (*supra*) an attempt was made to set up a custom that burgesses seised of shops adjoining the high street might sell their goods on market day in their shops.
[5] *Borough Customs*, II (S.S.), LXXVIII. [6] Clifton *v.* Chancellor, Mo. 624.

stepped[1]. It has been seen that in the seventh century purchases in London were specially favoured and though this special privilege seems for a time to have vanished, it reappeared when the doctrine of market overt was introduced by foreign merchants. The custom was gradually limited and defined, and it has been said that behind this process lies the whole history of the retail trade in London and of the special regulations concerning the place and manner of sale which were early established[2].

In 1455[3] we find a plea of purchase in market overt in the city of London, but there is no mention of the custom, and the case went on the point of good faith; two years later, in the case of the Crown Jewels[4], Fortescue, C.J., stated that it was said in the books and on the Bench that the people of London claim to have a market overt in every shop, " which God forbid! for every man could buy stolen goods secretly in his shop although the party had no time to take his goods or claim them and would be without remedy." In the great *Case of Market Overt* in 1595 the question was definitely raised. A scrivener pleaded in answer to a claim for restitution that he bought a basin and ewer in his shop and that the property was altered thereby. The town clerk said that it was usual to plead that each shop was a market overt for every saleable thing, but the court, like Fortescue, C.J., more than a century before, thought such a custom too wide, and too unreasonable to be deemed included in the confirmation of the liberties of the City by Parliament. They decided against the scrivener on the ground that each shop is a market overt only for such things as are accustomed to be sold therein and for no others[5]. Coke, in his report of the same case, says: " So every shop is a market overt for such things only which by the trade of the owner are put there to sale; and when I was Recorder of London, I certified the custom of London accordingly[6]."

Though the limitation of the doctrine to goods of the kind

[1] Norton, *Hist. of London* (3rd ed.), p. 161; L.Q.R. xxxi. p. 274.
[2] *Borough Customs*, II. *loc. cit.*
[3] Y.B. 33 H. VI. f. 5.　　　　　　　　　　　　　[4] Y.B. 35 H. VI. f. 25.
[5] Mo. 360 "pur tiels choses solement que sont uses d'estre achates et vendus en le shop, mes nemy pur auters choses."
[6] 5 Co. Rep. 83 b. Coke was Recorder in 1591 and 1592.

usually sold in the market has been chiefly discussed in relation
to the custom of London, it is, as Coke states, equally applicable to all markets overt in England. Its ground is thus stated
in Popham's[1] report of the case: "A scrivener's and cutler's
shop, or the like, is not proper for the sale of plate, nor a place
to which men will go to seek for such a thing lost or stole;
but a goldsmith's shop is the proper shop for it, as the draper's
shop is for woollen cloth, or the mercer's shop is for silk, and
the like: and to such men will go to seek for things of the
like nature that are lost or stolen, and not to a scrivener's shop
or the like." In *Taylor v. Chambers*[2] in the next reign the
shop of a person who was "of the mystery of mercers" was
held to be a market overt only for goods "agreeable to his
trade." Cheapside is not a market overt for horses, nor Smithfield for clothes.

The same reasons are at the bottom of the other rule, again
equally applicable to all markets, that the sale must be open
and in the open market[3]. In London, therefore, the sale must
be open and in an open shop, and in the *Case of Market Overt*
it seems to have been thought necessary that every passer-by
should be able to see the thing and also the sale of it. Thus
sales behind hangings or cupboards or in an inner room are
declared not to be open[4]. Whether the sale is open and in an
open shop is a question of fact in each case, so that no fixed
rule can be laid down. In *Lyons v. Le Pass*[5] a place described
by a witness as "an open warehouse with slippers in the
window" was found by the jury to be an open shop, Littledale, J.,
thinking that the openness necessary in former times was
impossible in later years and that it was a question of degree.
"It cannot be made a difficulty that there is now glass in the
window of shops, where in former times they were entirely

---

[1] Pop. 84; 5 Co. Rep. 83 b.

[2] Cro. Jac. 68.

[3] Coke, 2 Inst. 713, classes the rule as to the kind of goods under that pre-
scribing an "open place," "overt in this case implies apt and sufficient, as not to
sell plate in a scrivener's shop."

[4] Cf. City of London Case, 8 Co. Rep. 127, "secret places in corners are more
dangerous and offensive than outward shops, for there he may use deceit, and is
not subject to any search: qui male agit odit lucem, and omnia delicta in aperto
leviora sunt."

[5] 11 A. & E. 326.

open. Many shops are more open in their construction than others; but no difference can be made on that account." In *Hargreave v. Spink*[1], a sale in a show-room over a shop, to which customers were only admitted by special invitation was held not to be in market overt. It was said in a later case that a sale in such a place might be held to be open if there was a public notice of the sale to passers-by by placards, and to the world in general by advertisements; though whether the sale itself could be seen depended upon the amount of artificial light in the room and the light outside, and though none of the articles could actually be identified from outside[2]. On the other hand, mere publicity is not enough, so that a sale in a street outside a London shop, or in a public auction otherwise than in a shop is not a sale in market overt[3].

The change in conditions of trade may greatly modify the practical working of the custom, without actually altering it[4]. Thus the rise of the "general shop" may make the rule as to the class of goods almost a dead letter, and the general popularity of sales by auction may greatly widen the term "shop." Under statutes relating to the disturbance of markets, it has been held that premises do not cease to be a shop because auction sales take place there, though on the other hand, the mere fact that they are the private property of the person claiming them to be a shop and in his occupation, does not constitute them a shop[5]; and Lord Blackburn thought that "*prima facie* a sale by auction is not generally what you have in mind when speaking of selling in a shop[6]." Relying on these decisions Scrutton, J., in *Clayton v. Le Roy*[7] held that an auction room on the first floor of a building was not a shop, though he was careful not to say that no room or building in

---

[1] (1892) 1 Q.B. 25.
[2] Clayton *v.* Le Roy (1911), 2 K.B. 1031, 1045, per Scrutton, J., who thought the judges in Elizabeth's time would, in any case, have held the shop not to be an open one.
[3] Clayton *v.* Le Roy, *ib.* per Scrutton, J.; Cresswell, J., Lee *v.* Bayes, 18 C.B. 599, 601.
[4] See L.Q.R. XXXI. 287 as to whether the custom has been changed by the substitution of the usage of the particular shop-keeper for that of the trade, in determining the class of goods.
[5] Wiltshire *v.* Willett, 11 C.B. (N.S.) 240.
[6] Fearon *v.* Mitchell, L.R. 7 Q.B. 690.   [7] *Ubi sup.*

which auction sales are held can be a shop. In the room in question a counter separated the bidders from the auctioneer and no one staying behind this counter could see the articles sufficiently to examine them though they were allowed to see them by special permission. He was inclined to think that the judges in *Lyons v. Le Pass*[1] in holding a warehouse to be a shop had not merely extended the meaning of the term "shop" to meet modern conditions, but had modified the custom itself[2].

The custom of London, being in derogation, formerly of the custom of merchants, and now of the common law, is to be construed strictly and not to be extended to similar cases[3]. The Recorder of London, being a judge of the city, is supposed to have knowledge of its laws and customs, and by a special privilege certifies the custom into the King's Bench when it is tried as a question of law by the judges. If a party desires to have the custom so tried, he must conclude with a surmise that the custom ought to be tried by the certificate of the Recorder; otherwise, the custom is like the customs of other towns, which, "even those that are their local laws, are triable by jury, if they come to issue in the King's Courts[4]." The custom, being local, must be immemorial, and, therefore, it seems, can only be certified in the form mentioned by Coke.

The custom does not extend to protect pledges. In the *Case of the Crown Jewels*[5] the defendant's allegation that by the custom the pledgee might keep goods till the sum due was paid, was held contrary to reason, on the ground that the owner might have to refund to several sub-pledgees and might have to perform conditions other than the payment of money. In *Hartop v. Hoare*[6] it was said that sales in market overt are encouraged, "because they are a circulation of property,

---

[1] 11 A. & E. 326.
[2] In Wilkinson v. King, 2 Camp. 335, a wharf was held not to be a shop, but the sale was not within the city.
[3] Hartop v. Hoare, 2 Str. 1187; Hargreave v. Spink (1892), 1 Q.B. 25, 31, 32; Clayton v. Le Roy (1911), 2 K.B. 1031: "A custom which takes away one man's property and gives it to another must, in my view, be carefully watched," per Scrutton, J., at p. 1044; also per Fletcher Moulton, L.J., at p. 1047.
[4] Day v. Savadge, Hob. 85, citing Bilford v. Lowe, 37 & 38 Eliz. rot. 418; L.Q.R. XXXI. p. 277; Viner, Abr. *Custom*, pl. 2, 4, 5; Y.B. 11 Ed. IV. 3 per Littleton, J.
[5] Y.B. 35 H. VI. f. 25.   [6] 2 Str. 1187.

whereas pawning is *pro tem.* a locking of it up." The true
ground probably is that pledges, like gifts, were not transactions usual at fairs or markets; and this reasoning would
apply to the country as well as to London[1].

As part of the element of publicity required to bring a
transaction within the protection of a sale in market overt the
goods themselves must be present in the market[2]. "In order
to constitute a good sale in market overt, so as to pass the
property against the true owner, you must have the sale from
its commencement to its completion taking place in market
overt[3]." In *Hill v. Smith*[4] Mansfield, C.J., said that all the
doctrine of sales in market overt and of the court of Pie-
poudré was contrary to the notion of a sale by sample and
it has frequently been held that no tolls are due when goods
are not exposed for sale in the market[5]. The production of
a sample is not for this purpose a production of the bulk,
"for no fiction or intendment of law, no symbolical transfer
whatever, can operate to produce an effect merely material,
which can only be produced by natural means, namely, by
the specific production of the commodity itself in its proper
form and bulk[6]." On the other hand, a sale which is in the
market for the purpose of payment of toll may not be considered sufficient to pass the property against the true owner.
Thus the production and delivery of goods in the market, in
pursuance of an agreement made outside the market the day
before when the buyer, on payment of earnest, was given a
day to decide whether he would stick to his bargain, was held
insufficient to pass the property, on the ground that the delivery related back to the agreement[7]. There must, in fact, be

[1] Smith, *Mercantile Law* (11th ed.), Introd. LXXI.; Coke, 2 Inst. 713; City
Bank *v.* Barrow, 5 App. Cas. 664, 671, per Lord Selborne, "People do not give
security for money borrowed, in a fair or market."   [2] Y.B. 12 Ed. IV. 8.
[3] Cockburn, C.J., Crane *v.* London Dock Co., 33 L.J. Q.B. 224.
[4] 4 Taunt. 533.
[5] Leight *v.* Pym, Lut. 1329; Kirby *v.* Wichelow, Lut. 1498; Wells *v.* Miles,
4 B. & Ald. 559.
[6] Bailiffs of Tewkesbury *v.* Diston, per Ellenborough, C.J., 6 East 438 at
p. 459.
[7] Dyer, 1 Mar. 99 (68); 2 Rolle, Abr. *Market* (E), p. 124. It was thought
that the vendor was bound to keep the bargain open by the payment of five shillings.
See Barker *v.* Reading, W. Jones, 163. "Si agreement hors de Markett, et ceo
apres ratifie en le market: en tout ceux cases le property n'est alter."

a "sale" within the Sale of Goods Act, 1893, and not merely an agreement to sell, or a delivery of the goods[1].

From the case mentioned in the St Ives Fair Roll in 1291 down to the present day, most of the reported decisions deal with purchases by the proprietor of the place for which the privilege was claimed, but till the case of *Crane v. London Docks Co.*[2] it was never suggested that such a sale was unprotected. Cockburn, C.J., in that case thought the fact that the point was never raised an argument against its tenability, though he himself thought it "a proposition of very considerable difficulty and nicety"; Blackburn, J., thought it depended upon the question "whether it is usage or custom of the shop—the trade of the shop—to make it a place for the purchase of commodities brought there, and exposed there in specie to the shopkeeper for purchase"; but as the sale was by sample it was unnecessary to decide the point. In *Hargreave v. Spink*[3], Wills, J., thought that the custom of London did not cover a sale to a shopkeeper, basing his opinion on the absence of any express decision and the tendency of the courts to restrict the custom. Here again the point was unnecessary for the decision, so that the matter is still in doubt. The above cases were on the custom of London, and it has never been suggested that such a sale in an ordinary market would not pass the property, but here also there is no express decision. It is possible that a different rule might be applied in the country; for, as Wills, J., pointed out, a shopkeeper has a more or less permanent status, whilst persons dealing in markets, and still more in fairs, in the country, meet together for the occasion at intervals[4].

Bad faith, here as elsewhere, prevents the passing of the property, though the rules as to the publicity of the transaction and the class of goods sold, go far to secure honesty

---

[1] Cf. Lambert *v.* Rowe (1914) 1 K.B. 38, where it was held that a "sale" under the Markets and Fairs Acts, 1847 (s. 13) was to be understood in a popular sense and not with reference to the "niceties" of the law of sale.

[2] 33 L.J. Q.B. 224, 227, 229.

[3] (1892) 1 Q.B. 25.

[4] Cf. Clifton *v.* Chancellor, Mo. 624, sale to a shopkeeper at Bristol, point not raised. The former opinion of judges that the vendor should be named in the writ might be urged as an argument against protecting such a sale. See 9 H. VI. 45 (b) per Paston and Newton, JJ.; and L.Q.R. *loc. cit.*

on the purchaser's side[1]. Even after a sale in market overt the goods can always be retaken from the wrongful taker; and the owner who finds he is purchasing his own goods in market overt is not bound to give the price unless the property has passed by a previous sale[2]. The sale does not protect a seller, even when innocent, who has not acquired the ownership[3]; nor does it bind the King[4], but it binds lunatics, infants and others of limited capacity unless they are known to the purchaser to be the owners[5]. By 1 Jac. I. c. 21, s. 5, a broker within the city of London or two miles therefrom can acquire no title; but the Act has been construed to apply to pawnbrokers only[6].

There is no market overt for ships. "A ship is not like an ordinary personal chattel; it does not pass by delivery, nor does the possession of it prove the title to it[7]." The common law rules have also been modified with respect to horses by 2 & 3 Ph. & M. c. 7 and 31 Eliz. c. 12 which enact that the property in horses is not altered even by a sale in market or fair unless the solemnities there prescribed are fulfilled. Thus the horse must be openly exposed for a time in the market and tolled for in the toll book, and the seller must bring a witness known to the toll-keeper to attest the sale. The non-observance of these formalities in any respect prevents the sale being considered in market overt[8], in the case of horses tortiously taken as well as stolen[9]; and the due observance of the conditions will not be presumed by the court in the absence of proof by the person who would have benefited by their fulfilment[10]. It seems that the purpose of the Act is to

---

[1] Co. 2 Inst. 713; Best, J., Freeman v. East India Co., 5 B. &. Ald. 617, 624.
[2] Y.B. 33 H. VI. 5, pl. 15, 34 H. VI. 10, pl. 21; Perk. 93; 2 Inst. 713; Black. *Comm.* II. 449.
[3] Ganley v. Ledwidge, Ir. Rep. 10 C.L. 33; Delaney v. Wallis, 14 L.R. Ir. 31.
[4] Willion v. Berkley, Plowd. 223, 243.
[5] Co. 2 Inst. 713.
[6] This seems to imply that the rule applies to a sale to a shopkeeper.
[7] Hooper v. Gomm, 1866, 2 Ch. 282, 290 per Turner, L.J. In Wookey v. Pole, 4 B. & Ald. 16, Bayley, J., thought there could be a market overt for exchequer bills, *i.e.* the London Stock Exchange. Cf. Pollock, *Contracts* (8th ed.), p. 241: "Parties cannot set up a market overt for contractual rights."
[8] Gibb's Case, 1 Leon. 158; cf. Cro. Eliz. 86.
[9] Barker v. Reading, W. Jones 163.
[10] Moran v. Pitt, 42 L.J., Q.B. 47.

check fraudulent sales not purchases. Thus, a bona fide purchaser from one who had bought (as the second purchaser knew) at a fair on credit, without any evidence that he knew it was obtained dishonestly, was held entitled to maintain trover against the original owner for retaking it, although it did not appear that the formalities required by the statute had been complied with; and it may be that the result would have been the same if it had been proved that the first buyer had intended to defraud the owner[1]. By 31 Eliz. c. 12, s. 4, a sale which satisfies the requirements shall not take away the owner's title, if he claims the horse within six months before certain officials or justices and offers the possessor the price paid by him. The old system of *retrait*, which gave the purchaser an option to buy back the goods, has, therefore, only survived in our law in the case of horses. This provision only applies to stolen horses and in order that the magistrate before whom the complaint is made shall have jurisdiction to order the seizure of the horse from a bona fide purchaser, the owner "must lay a ground for the jurisdiction of the magistrate in an actual felony." The mere making of the complaint is not enough for this purpose, though it is sufficient to justify the issue of a warrant to apprehend the party charged with the felony *and* to take the property[2]. The rules relating to horses are in other respects similar to those governing the sale of other chattels. "If a man steale a horse and sell him in Smithfield, the true owner is barred by this sale; but if he sell the horse in Cheapside, Newgate or Westminster market, the true owner is not barred by this sale, because these markets are usual for flesh, fish, etc. and not for horses[3]."

According to Coke[4], "the common law did hold it for a point of great policy, and behoveful for the common-wealth, that fairs and markets overt should be replenished and well furnished with all manner of commodities vendible in fairs and markets for the necessary sustentation and use of the people" and he gives this as the reason and justification for the rule

---

[1] North v. Jackson, 2 Fost & F. 198.
[2] Joseph v. Adkins, 2 Stark. 76, 79, "He had a warrant against the man only, and this did not justify him in seizing the horse."
[3] Bacon, *Use of the Law*, p. 63.   [4] 2 Inst. 713.

of market overt. The protection would be all the more
necessary in former times if it were true that the common law
recognized no implied warranty of title on the sale of chattels,
and there is no doubt that in these days it has lost much of
its importance. That the rule is not altogether in harmony
with modern views in England may be seen from the fact that
the section dealing with the subject (s. 22) in the Sale of Goods
Act, 1893, was deleted by the Select Committee of the Commons
and the following substituted: "The buyer of goods in market
overt shall not acquire any better or other title thereto than if
the sale had taken place not in market overt"; and the ground
on which the original section was restored in Committee of
the whole House,—that so important a change in the law
endangered the passing of the Bill,—leaves unsettled the
expediency and justice of the rule itself[1].

The rule is accepted in Ireland but is alien to the law of
Scotland[2]. In the Scotch case of *Todd v. Armour*[3] a farmer
in Ireland brought an action against a farmer in Scotland for
delivery of a horse which the former alleged had been stolen
from him in Ireland. The defendant stated that the horse had
been bought by him in Scotland, at Falkirk Tryst, from a
man who had purchased it in market overt at Armagh Fair
in Ireland. The Court decided for the defendant on the ground
of the passing of the property by the sale in market overt in
Ireland but thought it unreasonable to require a Scotch court
to protect the possession of a purchaser in market overt in
Armagh, and refuse protection to a purchaser in market overt
at Falkirk[4]. The Lord Justice Clerk thought a question might
be raised as to the right of the real owner to receive his horse
back on paying to the bona fide purchaser his price; as to the
policy of the rule he thought that "the system of a *vitium reale*
which can never be removed, attaching to stolen property, is
preferable to that obtaining in England and Ireland." The

---

[1] Brown, *Sale of Goods Act*, p. 112. That it gives little real protection is seen
by the necessity for the Factors' Acts.
[2] See Bell's *Principles* (10th ed.), sec. 527. Sec. 22 of the Sale of Goods Act
does not apply to Scotland.
[3] (1882) 9 R. (C.S.) 901.
[4] See per Lord Young, p. 907.

doctrine has never been accepted in the United States[1], though it has sometimes been unsuccessfully urged that a bona fide purchaser in the usual course of trade is similarly protected ; moreover, it has been criticized " as contrary to honesty and the soundest policy[2]."

In France, as has been seen, not only a purchaser in a fair or market, but anyone buying in a public sale, or from a shop-keeper dealing in similar goods, can claim the return of the purchase money from the owner before giving up the goods[3]. By the law of Germany ownership may be acquired of goods stolen, lost, or otherwise missed, by a sale by public auction in the manner prescribed[4], but there does not seem to be any special recognition of sales in market overt[5].

(ii) ESTOPPEL.

By the Sale of Goods Act, 1893, s. 21, a person may give a better title than he has if the owner is "by his conduct precluded from denying the seller's authority to sell." This is usually classed as an example of the doctrine of estoppel, so called, according to Coke[6] " because a man's own act or acceptance stoppeth or closeth up his mouth to allege or plead the truth"; and it has been described as a device resorted to by the common law courts in order to "strengthen and lengthen their arm" by introducing equitable principles through the instrumentality of the rules of pleading[7]. The basis of the rule is therefore common to law and equity[8] being "the great principle of justice, that if one by his acts, or silence, or negligence, misleads another, or in any manner affects a transaction whereby an innocent person suffers a loss, the blameable party must bear it[9]." The blame,

[1] Ventress v. Smith, 10 Pet. (U.S.) 161, 176; Wheelwright v. Depeyster (N.Y.) 1 Johns 471, 3 Am. Dec. 345, per Kent, C.J.
[2] Duncan, J., Easton v. Worthington, 5 Serg. & R. 131, 25 Am. Dec. 609.
[3] S. 2280 of French Civil Code. The Canadian Code (art. 1489) alters "marchand" into "commerçant" but protects a sale "if it be a commercial matter." See City Bank v. Barrow, 5 App. Cas. 664, 671, where Lord Blackburn remarked that the French rule, though an extension of the rule of market overt, did not go much beyond the custom of London.
[4] Civil Code, arts. 935, 383.
[5] It is said in Y.B. 34 H. VI. f. 10, 21 that offering goods to an image operated like a sale in market overt to pass the title.
[6] Co. Lit. 352a.
[7] Bacon, V.-C., Keate v. Phillips, 18 Ch. D. 560, 577.
[8] Jorden v. Money, 5 H.L.C. 185 per Cranworth, L.C., p. 210.
[9] Garrard v. Haddon, 67 Pa. St. 82, at p. 85.

such as it is, generally attaches not in the original transaction, but later, and consists only in the fact that the owner "would, unless estopped, be saying something contrary to his former conduct in what he had said or done, or failed to say or do[1]." Blame which arises only because a person has failed to provide against an abnormal condition of things, such as fraud or forgery, is very near to innocence; and consequently, where the goods have been improperly obtained by the third party, the term "estopped," as implying fault, has been thought unsuitable[2].

The doctrine has been said to be more properly described as an instance of the general rule laid down by Ashhurst, J., in *Lickbarrow v. Mason*[3] "that whenever one of two innocent persons must suffer by the acts of a third, he who has enabled such third person to occasion the loss must sustain it"; or as it was put in an American case[4] often cited in English courts: "he shall suffer who by his indiscretion has enabled such third person to commit the fraud." The Sale of Goods Act uses the term "precluded" in place of "estopped."

The position of the purchaser, whether he be said to be "estopped" or "precluded," depends upon a common law rule of evidence[5], and, in theory, he is not considered to have acquired any title. Thus Brett, L.J., in *Sim v. Anglo-American Telegraph Co.*[6] said that an estoppel gives no title to that which is the subject matter of the estoppel; and *Richards v. Johnston*[7], where it was held that the sheriff was not bound by an estoppel, on the ground that he was not a party or privy to it, shews that the ownership of goods is not transferred by the rule of evidence. "The *fi. fa.* directs the sheriff to seize the goods of the debtor. The sheriff is a stranger to the debtor and the only question for him is—'Are these goods the goods of the debtor or not?'[8]" Had the property passed the sheriff would have been

---

[1] Bramwell, L.J., Baxendale v. Bennett 3, Q.B.D. 525, 529.
[2] Lord Campbell, C.J., Howard v. Hudson, 2 E. & B. 1, 10; Vaughan Williams, L.J., Fry v. Smellie (1912), 3 K.B. 282, 293.
[3] 1 Sm. L.C. 734.
[4] Root v. French (N.Y.), 13 Wend. 570, 572, per Savage, C.J.
[5] Bateman v. Faber (1898), 1 Ch. 144, 150; Williams v. Pinckney (1896), 67 L.J., Ch. 34, 37.
[6] 5 Q.B.D. 188, 206.   [7] 4 H. & N. 660.
[8] Per Martin, B. p. 664; cf. per Watson, B. p. 665, "though B may be

bound. But it is obvious that a rule, which prevents the owner from asserting his rights, in effect takes them from him and transfers them to the purchaser: and it is for this reason that estoppels are said to be "odious" and only employed by the courts with reluctance.

When the true owner is barred from claiming his property the question is not whether the wrongful vendor has authority to dispose of it, but whether the owner must be taken to have assented to the disposition; the purchaser's rights (for their existence cannot be denied) "are derived from the act of the real owner, which precludes him from disputing…the existence of the title or power which, through negligence or mistaken confidence, he caused or allowed to appear to be vested in the party making the conveyance[1]." It follows, therefore, that the rule of estoppel, as a common law doctrine, "needs no assistance from the equitable doctrine of bona fide purchasers for value without notice," which bases the purchaser's superior title upon the inherent strength of his own position and not upon the acts of the original owner[2].

According to Coke, estoppels were of three kinds, record, writing, and matter in *pais* and the acts coming under the third class were few and well defined, e.g. livery, entry, acceptance, partition[3]. The modern common law doctrine as applied to the purchase of goods dates from the case of *Pickard v. Sears*[4] in 1837, though the doctrine of admission by conduct had already been recognized by the common law courts[5]. One important difference between this and the old kinds of estoppel was that it might be used in evidence without being specially pleaded; but it seems that under the modern rules it is advisable, if not necessary, to raise on the pleadings the facts alleged to constitute the estoppel[6].

estopped, there was no transfer of any kind…therefore the property did not pass." This could only arise in practice where the goods were not in the purchaser's possession.

[1] McNeil *v.* Tenth Nat. Bank, 7 Am. Rep. 341, per Rapallo, J.; also Woodley *v.* Coventry, 2 H. & C. 164, per Martin, B.

[2] Lord Herschell in Bloomenthal *v.* Ford (1897), A.C. 156.

[3] Co. Lit. 352a; Ashburner, *Equity*, p. 629.   [4] 6 A. & E. 469.

[5] Heane *v.* Rogers, 9 B. & C. 577; Graves *v.* Key, 3 B. & Ad. 318 (a), "an admission is not so strong as an estoppel"; Richards *v.* Johnston, 4 H. & N. 660.

[6] 2 Sm. L.C., p. 866; Strode and Everest on Estoppel, p. 459; R.S.C., Order 19, R. 15.

In *Pickard v. Sears* the plaintiff's goods in the possession of a third party were seized under an execution against such third party and sold to the defendant. It was held that the jury might infer that the plaintiff authorized the sale from the fact that he consulted with the execution creditor as to the disposal of the property, without mentioning his own claim, after he knew of the seizure and of the intention to sell. Lord Denman stated the rule thus: "Where one by his words or conduct wilfully causes another to believe the existence of a certain state of things and induces him to act upon that belief, so as to alter his own previous position, the former is concluded from averring against the latter a different state of things as existing at the same time." In the later case of *Gregg v. Wells*[1], *G*, the owner of the fittings of a house, demised them to *D*, who thereupon became tenant to a third party, under an agreement giving the landlord a lien on the fittings, *G* being present at the execution of the agreement. *D* afterwards sold them without *G*'s knowledge to *W* who, being told by the landlord that *D* was his tenant, bought them in good faith. It was held that *G* could not claim them.

Just as in *Pickard v. Sears* the court thought that the owner's conduct in "standing by and giving a kind of sanction" to the seizure was a fact from which the jury might infer that he had ceased to be the owner, so in *Gregg v. Wells* it was laid down that the owner who "stands by and allows another to contract on the faith and understanding of a fact which he can contradict, cannot afterwards dispute that fact in an action against the person whom he has himself assisted in deceiving." The same idea lies at the root of the old equitable doctrine of "standing by[2]"—that a person who sees another about to commit, or in the course of committing, an act infringing upon his rights, cannot be heard to complain of the act if he stands by in such a manner as to induce the person committing it to believe that he assents to the commission. In many cases it is described as estoppel by acquiescence but it must be more than mere omission to act and must amount

---

[1] 10 A. & E. 90.
[2] See Hunsden *v.* Cheyney, 2 Vern. 150; Savage *v.* Foster, 9 Mod. 35.

to "acquiescence in such circumstances as that assent may be reasonably inferred from it[1]."

The owner is, therefore, only bound when his acts amount to a representation. This has led to the view that the rule is based upon an implied contract or licence[2], an opinion emphatically repudiated by Lord Selborne[3], but there is an obvious similarity to contract for there must be a "holding out" of the vendor, as having power to dispose of the goods, to a definite person (the purchaser) and not merely a "holding out to the world[4]." The representation may be wilful or negligent and may in either case consist of words or conduct. "A man may act so negligently that he must be deemed to have made a representation, which in fact he did not make, but because he has acted negligently he is deemed to have made it[5]"; and in *Carr v. L. & N. W. Co.*[6], Brett, J., defined estoppel by representation to include such conduct as a reasonable man would take to mean a representation.

In *Pickard v. Sears*, it is true, Lord Denman spoke only of "wilful" conduct but in *Gregg v. Wells* he applied the same principle to "a party who negligently or culpably stands by." The well-known case of *Freeman v. Cooke*[7], where the question was fully discussed, was one of trover by the assignee of a bankrupt against a sheriff for the conversion of the bankrupt's goods seized under a *fi. fa.* against *C* and *D*. It appears that immediately before the seizure the bankrupt told the officer that the goods were the property of *C* and then at once contradicted his former statement and said they were the goods of *D*. Parke, B., explained the rule in *Pickard v. Sears* thus: "By the term 'wilfully' however in that rule, we must understand, if not that the party represents that to be true which he knows

---

[1] De Bussche *v.* Alt, 8 Ch. D. 286, 314.
[2] Parke, B., Freeman *v.* Cooke, 2 Exch. 654, 662; Pollock, C.B., Cornish *v.* Abington, 4 H. & N. 549, 555.
[3] Citizens Bank of Louisiana *v.* Nat. Bank of New Orleans, L.R. 6 H.L. 352, 360; there is a likeness to contract in the fact that a person under disability cannot be estopped, Cannan *v.* Farmer, 3 Ex. 698.
[4] "A very loose expression," Dickinson *v.* Valpy, 10 B. & C. 140.
[5] Bell *v.* Marsh (1903), 1 Ch. 528, 541 per Collins, M.R.
[6] L.R. 10 C.P. 307, 317.
[7] (1848) 2 Ex. 654, see also per Denman, C.J., Coles *v.* Bank of England, 10 A. & E. 437, 451.

to be untrue, at least that he means his representation to be
acted upon, and that it is acted upon accordingly: and if, whatever a man's real intention may be, he so conducts himself that
a reasonable man would take the representation to be true, and
believe that it was meant that he should act upon it, and did
act upon it as true, the party making the representation would
be equally precluded from contesting its truth, and conduct,
by negligence or omission, where there is a duty cast upon a
person by usage of trade or otherwise to disclose the truth,
may often have the same effect." These words have been frequently cited with approval and establish that the word " wilfully " in *Pickard v. Sears* is opposed to " involuntarily " not
" unintentionally[1]."

Estoppel may therefore result from words or conduct, intentional or negligent.

Where the goods are improperly obtained it is clear that
the question of intentional representation by words is hardly
likely to occur often. The doctrine of estoppel is usually in-
voked in order to supplement the common law doctrine of
fraud, this being perhaps the only case in which the doctrine
of "making representations good" has survived *Derry v. Peek*[2].
Freeman v. Cooke shews that it is not necessary that the owner
should have intended his statements to be acted upon, provided
he had reasonable grounds for supposing they would be acted
upon and it was reasonable that they should be. Thus in the
above case it was held that the finding of the jury that the
officer was induced to seize the goods by the false representations that they belonged to *C* did not estop the bankrupt and
his assignees from complaining of the seizure, on the ground
that no reasonable man would have acted upon statements so
contradictory[3].

The most obvious conduct by which the owner may hold
out another as having authority to dispose of goods is the intrusting him with them or with the documents relating to them;
but it has long been settled that mere possession of personal

[1] Cornish *v.* Abington, 4 H. & N. 549, 555; Jorden *v.* Money, 5 H.L.C. 185,
214; Citizens Bank of Louisiana *v.* Nat. Bank of New Orleans, L.R. 6 H.L. p. 360.
[2] Per Farwell, L.J., Fry *v.* Smellie (1912), 3 K.B. 282, 295.
[3] See also Low *v.* Bouverie (1891), 3 Ch. 82.

property does not convey a title to dispose of it. On the other hand "strangers can only look to the acts of parties and to the external indicia of property[1]." Thus, though a watchmaker to whom a watch is intrusted for repair is not exhibited to the world as owner nor is credit given him as possessor of the watch, yet where the person into whose name the owner transfers goods buys and sells such goods as part of his usual business, the owner is bound by his acts[2]. The common law doctrine of estoppel, therefore, did not go very far and after it had been settled that a factor had no authority to pledge[3], the Legislature intervened. The result was the series of Factors' Acts 1823–1877 now replaced by the Act of 1889[4]. This Act only applies where the goods, or documents of title to goods, are intrusted to the mercantile agent, so that it goes no further than the common law in protecting purchasers from sellers who have improperly obtained the goods—"intrusting" being essentially different from "enabling to obtain." But where the owner is induced by fraud to intrust his goods to the mercantile agent they may be said to be both intrusted and improperly obtained, and it has been held that the Acts apply though the intention of the owner that the agent should have possession has been induced by fraud[5]. A more difficult question arises where the fraud amounts to larceny by a trick, but, though the matter is doubtful, the weight of opinion seems to be against protecting the purchaser[6]. The effect at common law of merely intrusting another with a document of title to goods is seen in the law relating to bills of lading which have nōt even a "qualified

---

[1] Pickering v. Busk, 15 East 38, 43.
[2] Ib.; cf. Wilkinson v. King, 2 Camp. 335.
[3] Paterson v. Tash, 2 Str. 1178.
[4] 52 & 53 Vict. c. 45. For the history of the law on this subject see the judgment of Willes, J., Fuentes v. Montis, L.R. 3 C.P. 268, pp. 277, 278; also per Lord Herschell, Bank of England v. Vagliano (1891), A.C. 107, 149. The Act of 1889, unlike the previous acts, does not use the word "intrusted" but requires the mercantile agent to be in possession "with the consent of the owner." Channel, J. (1907), 1 K.B. p. 527, thought the meaning was precisely the same.
[5] Sheppard v. Union Bank, 7 H. & N. 661; Baines v. Swainson, 4 B. & S. 270; Oppenheimer v. Attenborough (1907), 1 K.B. 510.
[6] Collins, L.J., Cahn v. Pocket's Bristol Channel Co. (1899), 1 Q.B. 643; Kennedy, L.J., Oppenheimer v. Attenborough (1908), 1 K.B. 221, 232; Kennedy and Fletcher Moulton, L.JJ., Oppenheimer v. Frazer & Wyatt (1907), 2 K.B. 50, 71, 77. Cf. Channell, J. (1907), 1 K.B. 510, 519 contra. For the distinction between false pretences and larceny by a trick see Kenny, Criminal Law (7th ed.), pp. 206, 207, 241.

negotiability" in the sense that a person improperly obtaining, as distinct from one improperly disposing of them, can defeat the right of stoppage *in transitu*[1].

The group of cases relating to "standing by" are instances of estoppel by intentional conduct and the case is stronger where words are added as in *Pickard v. Sears*. The owner has been held to be estopped, in an American case, by permitting another to take out a licence for his cart in his own name[2].

But it is clear that in those rare cases where the purchaser of goods "improperly obtained" is allowed to keep them, the estoppel usually results from negligence. Ashhurst, J., in *Lickbarrow v. Mason*, suggested that merely "enabling" the sale is sufficient to bar the true owner, but *Root v. French*[3] added the requirement of indiscretion. This takes us only a little way further for there is no doubt that mere carelessness, which enables a party to take, and wrongfully dispose of, goods does not deprive the owner of his property. If it were so the old common law principle that the owner of goods cannot be deprived of them without his own consent would be abrogated. "The right of the true owner is not prejudiced or affected by his carelessness in losing the chattel, however gross it may have been[4]," and this fundamental principle cannot be avoided by recourse to the rules of estoppel. "Would it be contended that if he (the owner) kept his goods so negligently that a servant took them and sold them, he must be considered as having concurred in the sale, and so be disentitled to sue for their conversion on a demand and refusal[5]?" It was suggested by Vaughan Williams, L.J., as the limitation to the principle laid down by Ashhurst, J., that the owner's act must be intended by him to be acted upon by someone[6]. But this would be inapplicable to cases of negligent omission and there is no reason to think that the rules applicable to negligence in other branches

---

[1] Saltus *v.* Everett, 20 Wend. (N.Y.) 267, 32 Am. Dec. 541.
[2] McCauley *v.* Brown, 25 Am. Dec. 612 (n).
[3] (N.Y.) 13 Wend. 570, 572.
[4] Lord MacNaghten in Farquharson Bros. *v.* King (1902), A.C. 325, 335.
[5] Parke, B., giving the opinion of the judges, adopted by the House of Lords, in Bank of Ireland *v.* Evans' Trustees, 5 H.L.C. 389, 411, approved in Mayor etc. of Merchants of Staple *v.* Bank of England, 21 Q.B.D. 160, 171, 176, 177.
[6] Farquharson Bros. *v.* King (1901), 2 K.B. p. 713.

of the law are not equally effective here. Thus in *Swan v. North British Australasian Co.*[1] Blackburn, J., after quoting Parke, B., in *Freeman v. Cooke* placed the rule broadly on the principles of negligence. "A man who does not lock up his goods, which are consequently stolen, may be said to be negligent as regards himself, but inasmuch as he neglects no duty which the law casts on him, he is not in consequence estopped from denying the title of those who may have, however innocently, purchased these goods from the thief unless in market overt," and he added that "the neglect must be the proximate cause of leading the party into the mistake." The same rule applies when the wrongful vendor has obtained possession of the documents of title to goods as a result of the owner's carelessness for, like title deeds of land, they cannot be regarded as being in the eye of the law "analogous to fierce dogs or destructive elements, where from the nature of the thing the Courts have implied a general duty of safe custody on the part of the person having their possession or control[2]."

The questions whether there is a duty and whether the negligence is the proximate cause of the sale run into each other in most cases. Who is to have the right to retain the goods depends upon the circumstances of each individual case, and a judge, though he has to decide whether there is any evidence to go to the jury[3] cannot lay down what is negligence so as to bind their successors[4]. The negligence must, in short, amount to a "holding out" to the purchaser. This is the result of the case of *Farquharson Bros. v. King*[5], which is an excellent example of the inroads which the extension of the principle of estoppel might make upon the general principle of the non-negotiability of goods. Timber merchants warehoused with a dock company timber imported by them, and instructed the company to accept all transfer or delivery orders signed by their clerk who had authority to make limited sales to their

[1] 2 H. & C. 175.
[2] Longman v. Bath Electric Tramways Co. (1905), 1 Ch. 646, 665 per Romer, L.J., quoting Fry, L.J., Northern Counties &c. Co. v. Whipp, 26 Ch. D. 482, 493.
[3] Metropolitan Rly. Co. v. Jackson, 3 A.C. 193, 197, per Lord Cairns.
[4] See per Sankey, J., McMillan v. London Joint Stock Bank (1917), 1 K.B. 363, 367.
[5] (1902) A.C. 325.

known customers. The clerk, under an assumed name, fraudulently sold timber to bona fide purchasers, who knew nothing of the merchants or of the clerk under his real name. The clerk carried out the sale by orders in his real name into his assumed name and then in that name to the defendants. It was strongly argued in the Court of Appeal that, as the clerk was not held out to the defendants as having authority to dispose of the goods, judgment for the defendant would shew that the common law contained a principle going beyond, and rendering unnecessary, the Factors' Acts. It was nevertheless held by a majority of the Court that it was sufficient that the owner *enabled* the agent to hold himself out as entitled to dispose of the timber, though it was admitted that the consequence must not be too remote[1]. The House of Lords overruled this decision on the ground that the owner's title cannot be altered merely by his enabling another party to transfer possession of the goods to a bona fide purchaser; there must be something in the nature of "holding out" to the particular purchaser[2]. Lord Mac-Naghten explained the rule thus: "If I lose a valuable dog and find it afterwards in the possession of a gentleman who bought it from somebody whom he believed to be the owner, it is no answer to me to say that he never would have been cheated into buying the dog if I had chained it up or put a collar on it or kept it under proper control. If a person leaves a watch or a ring on a seat in the park or on a table at a café and it ultimately gets into the hands of a bona fide purchaser it is no answer to the true owner to say it was his carelessness and nothing else that enabled the finder to pass it off as his own. If that be so, how can carelessness, however extreme, in the conduct of a man's own business preclude him from recovering his own property which has been stolen from him?"

The last words appear to imply that there can be no estoppel when the improper taking amounts to theft, and this seems to have been the opinion of Lord Halsbury, L.C., who said:

---

[1] (1901) 2 K.B. 712.
[2] Lord Lindley (1902) A.C. p. 342 thought that the owner is not bound when nothing has been done by him which has in fact misled the purchaser. Cf. an article by Mr J. S. Ewart, L.Q.R. XVIII. p. 160 *sq.*

" I think it may be stated compendiously in two sentences. A servant has stolen his master's goods, and the question arises whether the persons who have received those goods innocently can set up a title against the master. I really do not understand what estoppel has to do with the case[1]." Again, in *Baxendale v. Bennett*[2], Bramwell, L.J., thought it was a rule "that everyone has a right to suppose that a crime will not be committed, and to act on that behalf." If there be such a rule it is clear that the application of the rules of estoppel, where goods are improperly obtained, will be very rare. But it seems to be equally clear that no such rule exists in English law and the cases upon which such a principle might be based can be explained on other grounds. Thus in one case[3], where the negligent custody of a common seal enabled a forgery to be committed, the decision was grounded on the principle that the negligence must be in, or immediately connected with the transfer to the innocent purchaser, so that the purchase was the necessary, or ordinary, or likely result of the negligence. Other cases have been decided on the ground that there was no legal duty to the public on the part of the owner to keep his own property safely[4]. Mr Beven's conclusion is that "where a duty exists antecedently to the commission of a crime, the fact that a crime is committed does not affect the liability flowing from the breach of duty. On the other hand, where there is no duty existing antecedently to the crime the fact that a crime results from lax dealing does not raise one."

In *Scholfield v. Earl Londesborough*[5], it was said that there is no duty to suppose that those against whose character there is no imputation will commit a crime whenever the opportunity occurs. There does not seem to be any case in which the owner of goods has been estopped when the improper obtaining has amounted to a crime, but it has frequently

---

[1] There was in fact no asportation sufficient to constitute larceny, see note by Sir F. Pollock, L.R. 1902 A.C. p. 329.
[2] 3 Q.B.D. 525, 530.
[3] Bank of Ireland v. Evans' Trustees, 5 H.L.C. 389.
[4] Patent Safety Gun Co. v. Wilson (1880), 49 L.J.Q.B. 713; Brown v. Bennett, 9 N.Z.L.R. (C.A.) 485 per Williams, J., p. 507, cited in Beven on Negligence (3rd ed.), p. 1324. See Blackburn, J., in Swan v. N. British Aust. Co., 2 H. & C. 181; Arnold v. Cheque Bank, 1 C.P.D. 578.
[5] (1896) A.C. 514, 544.

been suggested in cases concerning negotiable instruments that
there is a duty not to be negligent in trusting to the honesty
of servants. In *Arnold v. The Cheque Bank*[1] it was held that
the owner of property was not negligent in trusting servants
in the discharge of their ordinary duty of conveying letters to
the post, and that the post office was the recognized means of
transmitting letters with their contents except actual money.
It follows that there would be no negligence in sending parcels
of goods, at any rate within the prescribed limits as to weight
and size. It was suggested that a duty to the general public
would arise when one of the servants was a notorious thief[2];
and in the slightly later case of *The Patent Safety Gun etc. Co.
v. Wilson*[3] the bona fide holder of a cheque, which had been
stolen and forged pleaded that the forger, known to have been
convicted of embezzlement and to be a notorious thief, was
allowed access to the plaintiff's cheques. Grove, J., thought
the defence good as shewing a neglect of duty to the defendant
as one of the public. This was overruled by the Court of
Appeal on the ground that there was no relation between the
plaintiffs and the defendant, which could cause any duty to
exist between them.

The distinctions[4] which have been suggested as to the care
required when the goods can only be obtained by forgery and
not merely by larceny, can in the same way be subordinated
to the closely connected questions, whether there is a duty, and
whether the negligence is the proximate cause of the sale.
The above mentioned decisions shew that whilst it is theo-
retically possible that the owner may be estopped by his
negligence such cases when the goods are improperly obtained
are bound to be rare and are carefully watched by the Courts[5].

The purchaser, therefore, cannot say that he was induced
to act on the faith of the owner's conduct unless his purchase

---

[1] (1876) 1 C.P.D. 578.
[2] At p. 589 per Lord Coleridge, C.J.
[3] (1880) 49 L.J., Q.B. 713. Also Lewes Sanitary Laundry Co. *v.* Barclay & Co.
(1906), 95 L.T. 444.
[4] See Arnold *v.* The Cheque Bank, *ubi sup.*
[5] "There may, perhaps, be strong cases where the negligence of the owner
would be so gross as to so invite plunder that he might be regarded as a consenting
party and thus be deprived of all right of recovery." Pease *v.* Smith, 61 N.Y.
(16 Sick.) 477 at p. 486.

was its direct result. "It is the payment that creates the estoppel and if that is not made in reliance on the act of the owner, the latter is not, and cannot, in the nature of things, be estopped[1]." It is for the purpose of shewing that the purchase was thus induced that good faith is essential, for when the purchaser has suspicions as to the vendor's title he cannot be said to be misled by the owner's conduct. For the same reason the owner cannot be estopped by conduct subsequent to the purchase. Thus, in an American case, it was held that the mere fact that the owner of property, sold without authority to a bona fide purchaser, does not immediately seek to recover possession from the purchaser will not deprive him of his right to do so[2]; and though such sale is an infringement of his rights, when once the act is completed, without any knowledge or consent on his part, "mere submission to the injury for any time short of the period limited by statute for the enforcement of the right of action cannot take away such right, although under the name of laches, it may afford a ground for refusing relief under some particular circumstances[3]."

(iii) SALE BY VENDOR WITH VOIDABLE TITLE.

By a rule of the common law now codified in s. 23 of the Sale of Goods Act, 1893, a person who has a voidable title to goods can transfer to an innocent purchaser a better title than he himself has. The principle upon which the rule is based has been said to be "not that the second vendee had a good title, and therefore the first sale was not void, but that the first sale was not void, and therefore the second vendee had a good title[4]." According to this view the first vendee has a title analogous to that of a legal transferee of an estate subject to a trust, a bona fide purchaser in each case acquiring a good title free from latent claims. The objection that since the owner can bring trover against the fraudulent vendee the legal title must

---

[1] Barnard v. Campbell, 55 N.Y. 456, 465, 14 Am. Rep. 28, 37.

[2] Harrison v. Clark, 74 Conn. 18, delay of eight weeks after knowledge of sale, see 24 Am. & Eng. Encyc. of Law, 1061; McKenzie v. British Linen Co., 6 App. Cas. 82, silence for a fortnight after knowledge of forgery of bill; also De Gorter v. Attenborough, 21 T.L.R. 19.

[3] De Bussche v. Alt (1878), 8 Ch. D. 286 per Thesiger, L.J., p. 314.

[4] Billiter v. Young, 6 E. & B. p. 25 per Cresswell, J., referring to White v. Garden, 10 C.B. 919.

continue in the former, is met by the contention that such a plaintiff recovers on his equitable right to recover. Thus Prof. Ames says : " In truth, the fraudulent vendee who gets the legal title is a constructive trustee, and the action of trover against him presents the anomaly of a bill of equity in a court of common law[1]." In an American case[2], deciding that a bona fide second purchaser may recover from the seller the value of the chattels reclaimed from him by a fraudulent prior purchaser, whose title has not been disaffirmed and who has obtained possession of part of the goods, the decision was based upon the ground that the legal title had passed to the prior purchaser ; and, indeed, this is implied by the very use of the term "voidable title," by which is meant "a title, which if the person entitled to avoid, does not elect to avoid it, will be a good title[3]."

This view would differentiate this class of cases from those where the owner is estopped from asserting his rights and in which the legal title, as it were, jumps over the wrongful vendor, for there the purchaser bases his claim on the acts of the original owner. But in *Irving v. Motley*[4], Tindal, C.J., said : " There was an acting, and the appearance of purchase given to the transfer of these goods which in truth and justice it did not really possess "; and in a Scottish case[5] the rule of the English Courts was said to be based on the principle " that a purchaser is not bound to look beyond the ostensible title of possession, and that if the true owner have knowingly con- ferred this ostensible title, although induced thereto by fraud, a bona fide purchaser cannot be required to restore what he has bought." Many American cases also place the rule on this ground, the case of *Root v. French*[6], so often quoted in English cases relating to estoppel, being, in fact, one of a contract induced by fraud. These statements imply that the

---

[1] H.L.R. I. p. 424, n (2); also *Select Essays* &c., III. p. 445. In an article by Mr Z. Chafee, Jr., H.L.R. XXXI. p. 1115, the plaintiff's right is said to be based upon the principle in Duke of Somerset v. Cookson (1735), 3 P. Wms. 390 where it was held that a bill lay to compel the delivery of a curiosity in specie ; see also Gladstone v. Hadwen, 1 Mau. & S. 517, 527.

[2] Brown v. Pierce, 97 Mass. 46.

[3] Whitehorn Bros. v. Davison (1911), 1 K.B. 463, per Buckley, L.J., p. 481 ; Load v. Green (1846), 15 M. & W. 216, 223.

[4] 7 Bing. 543, 551.

[5] Brown v. Marr (1880), 7 R. 427, 436.

[6] 13 Wend. (N.Y.) 570.

vendor must have parted with the possession of the goods or the documents of title thereto, a limitation which does not seem to be recognized in our law[1]. Moreover the rule in *Cundy v. Lindsay*[2] that where the contract is void no title passes, seems to be against this view, for the principle of estoppel would, in many cases at least, apply as strongly where the contract is void as where it is voidable

The two views meet in the rules relating to rescission, by which act, according to the first, the owner revests the legal title in himself, or, according to the second, ceases to hold out the vendee as owner. These rules are based on equitable principles so far as the rights of third parties are concerned, and it has consequently been said that the rules relating to voidable contracts must resemble those of estoppel "so long as the rights based on each have the same equitable foundation[3]." In order to avoid the question it has been suggested that the term "estoppel" is better limited to "abnormal situations where the truth cannot be set up because of misconduct[4]."

The first case in which a good title was held to be transferred by a fraudulent vendee seems to be *Parker v. Patrick*[5], in 1793, in which it was decided that if goods are obtained from *A* by fraud, and pawned to *B* who takes in good faith, and *A* takes the goods from *B* after the conviction of the vendee, *B* may maintain trover for them. But the case went chiefly on the ground that a conviction for fraud is not on the same footing as one for larceny, and the wording of the judgment suggests that the Court thought the same rule would apply in the case of larceny but for a positive statute (that of restitution). Doubt was cast on the case by Lord Tenterden[6] on the ground that fraud would prevent the passing

---

[1] In those cases where the buyer or seller is estopped under the Factors' Act, 1889, and now under the Sale of Goods Act, 1893, s. 25, possession of goods or documents must be obtained or detained.

[2] 3 App. Cas. 459.

[3] Barnard *v.* Campbell, 58 N.Y. (13 Sick.) 73, 76, 17 Am. Rep. 208, 212.

[4] H.L.R. XXXI. p. 1119 (n).

[5] 5 T.R. 175.

[6] Earl of Bristol *v.* Wilsmore, 1 B. & C. 514; the property was to be paid for by ready money, but was delivered in return for a worthless cheque by a servant without authority. Lord Tenterden (then Abbot, C.J.) said that a preconceived design not to pay "would be such a fraud as would vitiate the sale, and according to the cases cited, would prevent the property from passing to him" (p. 521).

of the property, and by Lord Denman[1] on the question of the effect of a conviction for fraud[2]. But in *Load v. Green*[3], where the fraudulent vendee became bankrupt, and it was held that the goods were not in the order and disposition of the vendee with the consent of the true owner, as until the repudiation of the contract, the bankrupt was not only the apparent but the real owner, Parke, B., supported *Parker v. Patrick* for the reason that "the transaction is not absolutely void, except at the option of the seller; he may elect to treat it as a contract, and he must do the contrary before the buyer has acted as if it were such, and resold the goods to a third party." In *White v. Garden*[4] the modern rule was clearly laid down, the Court basing its decision on the judgment of Parke, B., in *Load v. Green*; and in the later case of *Stevenson v. Newnham*[5] the same eminent judge, after citing the above cases, said: "It must be considered, therefore, established that fraud only gives a right to avoid a contract or purchase; that the property rests until avoided; and that all mesne dispositions to persons not parties to, or at least not cognisant of, the frauds, are valid"; and again: "In the first instance the property passes in the subject matter. An innocent purchaser from the fraudulent possessor may acquire an indefeasible title to it though it is voidable between the original parties." The rule thus laid down has been frequently stated and acted upon[6].

As now understood, it is based upon the passing of the property until rescission, and is therefore equally applicable to cases where one person, induced by fraud, transfers goods to another *with the intention of vesting the property in him* although there may be no contract. Thus, where pledgees, as a result of fraudulent representations of the pledgors that they had sold the goods to the defendants, handed the pledgors

[1] Peer v. Humphrey, 2 A. & E. 495.
[2] See also Noble v. Adams, 7 Taunt. 59.
[3] (1846) 15 M. & W. 216, p. 219.
[4] (1851) 10 C.B. 919; Cresswell, J., based his opinion on the ground that of two innocent parties the negligent one should suffer.
[5] (1853) 13 C.B. 285, 302.
[6] See Kingsford v. Merry, 11 Ex. 577, 579, per Pollock, C.B.; Cundy v. Lindsay, 3 App. Cas. 459, 464 per Lord Cairns, L.C.; Moyce v. Newington, 4 Q.B. 32, 35 per Cockburn, C.J.; Rowley v. Bigelow, 29 Mass. 306, 312, 23 Am. Dec. 613 per Shaw, C.J.; Benjamin on Sale (5th ed.), p. 457.

the delivery order which enabled the defendants to obtain the goods, the case was considered analogous to that of a sale induced by fraud and the same principle was held to apply[1]. Similarly, the same principles would probably govern resales by fraudulent donees[2].

There must, however, either be privity of contract, which implies intention to pass the property, or such an intention independently of contract, for the second vendor must have a title, be it only a voidable one, vested in himself. The case of *Kingsford v. Merry*[3] shewed that there might be a transaction, at first sight very like a contract, which could not give even a voidable title. *L*, the purchaser of goods, endorsed the delivery orders specially to himself and delivered them to *A* to enable him to inspect the goods. *A* requested the delivery of the goods from the plaintiff saying that he had purchased them from *L*. After having the goods transferred to his name, he pawned them for a bona fide advance. In the Court of Exchequer Pollock, C.B., thought the rule in *White v. Garden* applicable, but was overruled in the Exchequer Chamber on the ground that "there was no privity of contract between them (the original owners) and *A*, and it was only as representing himself, as claiming under *L*, that they gave him by the delivery order the means of possessing the goods. Such a delivery, under the circumstances of this case, would no more pass the property in the goods, than a delivery to an agent or servant of *L* would pass the property to such servant." It followed that "mere possession with no further indicia of title than a delivery order" could not give the pawnee the right to resist an action of trover[4].

This principle was followed soon after in *Higgins v. Burton*[5] where a person, fraudulently representing that he was authorized

---

[1] Babcock *v.* Lawson (1878), 4 Q.B.D. 394 per Cockburn, C.J., it was assumed that the plaintiffs had originally a special property in the goods. The principle of Root *v.* French was also relied on as an independent ground.

[2] In equity (though not at law) a donor may recover his gift from the donee if induced even by *innocent* misrepresentations. In re Glubb (1900) 1 Ch. 354.

[3] (1857) 26 L.J. Ex. 83, 1 H. & N. 503; reversing (1856) 25 L.J. Ex. 166, 11 Ex. 577. See per Willes, J., in Fuentes *v.* Montis, L.R. 3 C.P. 268 as to the discussion caused by the case.

[4] (1857) 26 L.J. Ex. p. 89.

[5] (1857) 26 L.J. Ex. 342.

J.   5

by another to purchase goods, induced the owner to deliver them to him, in the belief that he was transferring the ownership to the alleged principal; and in the well-known case of *Hardman v. Booth*[1] where the plaintiff, dealing with a man named Edward Gandell, was led by him to believe that he was one of the firm of Gandell and Company, an innocent purchaser was again held to acquire no title. These cases differ from *Kingsford v. Merry* as there was no contract at all with the persons mentioned as principals, but they all rest on the ground that the fraudulent party is merely a tortious possessor who does not come within the contemplation of the owner as a party to the contract. The position was clearly shewn in a case where the goods sent to the firm mentioned were refused, and were then delivered by the carrier at the supposed agent's request to a bona fide purchaser[2]. In each case the fraudulent person is merely a tortious holder of the goods.

These cases are therefore based on the absence of a contract between the parties, for when the misrepresentation relates to so material a fact as the identity of the other party "there is merely the one side to a contract, where, in order to produce a contract, two sides would be required[3]." This is clearly seen in the well-known case of *Cundy v. Lindsay*[4] where there was no question of agency at all and the fraudulent person and the owner were not face to face[5]. The respondents were induced, by the fraud of Blenkarn, who ordered goods from them under a name so written as to appear to be Blenkiron, the name of a highly respectable firm well known to the respondents, to send the goods addressed to Blenkiron which were received by Blenkarn. Blackburn, J., while agreeing that the decision in *Hardman v. Booth* was good law, held it inapplicable in the circumstances of the case; but his view was not accepted by the Court of Appeal nor by the House of

---

[1] 1 H. & C. 803. See also Hollins *v.* Fowler, L.R., 7 H.L. 757 considered by the Queen's Bench and House of Lords to be indistinguishable from Hardman *v.* Booth.

[2] Moody *v.* Blake, 117 Mass. 23; 19 Am. Rep. 394.

[3] (1878) 3 App. Cas. 459, 465.   [4] *Ib.*

[5] In a very recent case Horridge, J., has held that a purchaser who *in person* obtains goods by pretending to be another acquires a voidable title. Phillips *v.* Brooks, Ltd. (1919), 2 K.B. 243 approving Edmunds *v.* Merchants' Despatch Transport Co. 135 Mass. 283.

Lords which held that the goods were recoverable from a
bona fide purchaser from Blenkarn, on the ground that there
was no contract between the latter and the respondents. "Of
him they knew nothing, and of him they never thought. With
him they never intended to deal. Their minds, never, even for
an instant of time, rested upon him, and as between him and
them there was no consensus of mind, which could lead to any
agreement or any contract whatever[1]."

The result has been thus summed up in a later Scottish
case[2]: "If a man obtains goods by pretending to be somebody
else[3], or by pretending that he is an agent for somebody, who
has in fact given him no authority, there is no contract between
the owner of the goods and him; and there is no consensus
which can support a contract." A sub-purchaser in good faith,
therefore, cannot keep the goods.

This effect is produced whenever a contract is void from
any cause, e.g., it formerly occurred under the old law of usury,
which rendered the contract void ab initio[4]. Therefore, it is
important to know (i) whether a contract is void ab initio or
voidable[5]; and (ii) when a voidable contract becomes void, i.e.
when rescission of a voidable contract is possible.

(i) It has been seen that where the misrepresentation concerns the identity of one of the parties the contract is void ab
initio. On the other hand, the mere fact that the purchaser has
been guilty of fraud is not always enough to render the contract voidable; the fraud must have induced the vendor to

[1] Per Lord Cairns, L.C. p. 465; also Baillie's Case (1898), 1 Ch. 110. See the
earlier case of Duff v. Budd, 3 Brod. & B. 177 which, if it can be supported, rests
on the failure of the property to pass to a person not in the vendor's contemplation.
Benjamin on Sale (5th ed.), p. 457 n (3).
[2] Morrison v. Robertson (1908), S.C. 332, 339, per Lord Kinnear. Sect. 23 of
the Sale of Goods Act applies to Scotland.
[3] See p. 66 n (5).
[4] Tregoning v. Attenborough, 7 Bing. 97, 99, where it was said: "In trover the
question is one of strict legal title; and if the contract be usurious the defendant's
title fails." See as to the imposition of equitable terms, Lodge v. Nat. Union Co.
(1907), 1 Ch. 300, 312, per Parker, J. The Money-lenders Act, 1911 (1 & 2
Geo. V. c. 38, s. 1) validates bona fide payments or transfers of money or property
by third persons on the faith of the validity of any agreement rendered void by
the Money-lenders Act, 1900 (63 & 64 Vict. c. 51, s. 2 (1)).
[5] In Baillie's Case (1898), 1 Ch. 110, 114, a distinction was drawn between "a
contract...voidable...on the ground of misrepresentation" and "something which
was void ab initio."

enter into the contract. Thus of the two kinds of fraud (i) quod causam dedit contractui, (ii) quod tantum in contractum incidit, it is the material, and not the merely incidental fraud which renders the contract voidable[1]. The circumstance about which the vendor is likely to be most concerned is the purchaser's intention to pay for the goods, and in *Earl of Bristol v. Wilsmore*[2] and *Ferguson v. Carrington*[3], Lord Tenterden thought it so important, that he seems to have had some doubt as to whether even a voidable title would pass to the purchaser, when the owner was wilfully deceived in this respect. It has, however, long been settled that fraudulent misrepresentation here also renders the contract voidable not void.

A wilfully false statement would be a clear ground for avoiding the sale but it is well established that a silent preconceived design not to pay for them has the same effect[4]. In a recent Scottish case it was said: " It has been repeatedly decided that to buy goods with the intention of not paying for them is a fraud going to the foundation of the contract, and if that fraudulent intention were proved against the buyer, I apprehend it would not be necessary to go further and inquire into any particular statements and representations which may have been made by him to the vendor, because his conduct in buying is itself a representation that he intends to pay; and it must always be presumed that the seller parts with his goods only in the expectation of being paid for them[5]." The usual method of proving this mental state is to shew that the purchaser could have had no reasonable expectation of paying for them, *e.g.*, where he was on the verge of insolvency, or where immediately after receiving them he sold at once at greatly reduced prices[6].

But the mere fact that the vendee is in embarrassed circumstances is no proof of fraud where the goods are handed over

[1] In the words of Lord Ellenborough the Court "cannot try a question of warranty in an action of trover," Emanuel *v.* Dane, 3 Camp. 299.
[2] 1 B. & C. 514.   [3] 9 B. & C. 59.
[4] Irving *v.* Motley, 7 Bing. 543; Load *v.* Green, 15 M. & W. 216; In re Eastgate (1905), 1 K.B. 465.
[5] Gamage, Ltd. *v.* Charlesworth's Trustee, 1910, S.C. 257, 264, per Lord Kinnear ; also Hart *v.* Moulton, 104 Wis. 349, 76 Am. St. Rep. 881.
[6] Ferguson *v.* Carrington, 9 B. & C. 59; this would be of no use against a bona fide purchaser.

on credit. " When a man sells goods, he sells them on the credit of the buyer; if he delivers the goods the property is altered, and he cannot recover them back again, though the vendee immediately becomes bankrupt[1]." In *Ex parte Whittaker*[2] a purchaser bought wool at an auction a few days after committing an act of bankruptcy by non-compliance with a debtor's summons for a small debt. The vendor being unaware of his embarrassed circumstances allowed him to take it away shortly afterwards without paying for it and without his making any representation as to payment. The purchaser was subsequently adjudged bankrupt without taking any steps to oppose the adjudication; he had not sold the wool nor attempted to raise money on it. It was held that the evidence was insufficient for assuming that the purchaser did not intend to pay for the goods. In the Court of Appeal it was admitted that the purchaser must be taken to have made an implied representation as to his intention to pay for the goods but that his intent not to do so was not clearly made out. "A man buying is not bound to tell all his affairs to those with whom he deals, though he must not say anything which amounts to a misrepresentation." But if a man orders goods to be sent to him at night, and early the next morning commits an act of bankruptcy he must be taken to have obtained possession "by artifice or fraud[3]." It has been held in an Irish case that, where the purchaser in a sale for ready money knows he has no funds at the bank, a giving of a cheque is a false representation of a material fact, which entitles the seller to rescind, though the purchaser believed on reasonable grounds that the cheque would be paid[4].

" To authorize the rescission of a sale of chattels on the ground of fraud on the part of the vendee, so that a recovery may be had in detinue or trover against the first purchaser or sub-purchaser[5], these conditions or facts must be combined:

[1] Lickbarrow *v.* Mason, 1 Sm. L.C. 726, 734, per Ashhurst, J.
[2] 10 Ch. 446, 449.
[3] Sinclair *v.* Stevenson, 10 Mo. 46, 53 per Best, C.J., Durrell *v.* Haley, 19 Am. Dec. 444.
[4] Loughnan *v.* Barry, I.R. 6 C.L. 457.
[5] *I.e.* in bad faith.

(1) The purchaser must, at the time of the transaction, have been insolvent or in failing circumstances; (2) The purchaser must have had either a pre-conceived design not to pay for the goods or no reasonable expectation of being able to pay for them[1]; (3) The purchaser must have intentionally concealed these facts or made a fraudulent representation in regard to them; (4) the sale must have been induced by the fraudulent representation or concealment[2]."

A contract induced by duress is in the same way voidable not void[3].

(ii) The result of rescinding a contract is to divest the property from the vendee to the vendor; the contract ceases to exist and the vendee becomes a tortious holder liable for conversion[4]. So long as the contract continues to subsist the vendor cannot claim the goods, and therefore it is necessary to examine the limitations to his right of rescission where the conduct of the vendee at the time of the sale has been of a nature to enable him to use this right. The most important principle, recognized at law and in equity, is that as a condition precedent to a rescission a *restitutio in integrum* must be possible[5]. It is on this ground that rescission is impossible when the goods have already been transferred to a bona fide purchaser. "The rule of law has been thoroughly established, that where a contract is voidable on the ground of fraud, you may avoid it, so long as the goods remain in the man's hands who is guilty of the fraud, or in the hands of anybody who takes them from him with notice; but where a person has bona fide acquired an interest in the goods, you cannot, as against that person, avoid

---

[1] The absence of reasonable expectation would in this country probably only be evidence of a preconceived design not to pay.

[2] Pelham v. Chattahoochee Grocery Co. (1906), 119 Am. St. Rep. 19 (146 Ala. 216), a decision stated by the court to be based on rules "announced by this court in a series of cases which seem plainly to settle the law on the subject and to indicate the scope and nature of the inquiry."

[3] See Pollock on Contracts, p. 636. Duress which excluded consent and therefore contract would amount to obtaining possession by intimidation within the Larceny Act, 1916 (6 & 7 Geo. V. c. 50, s. 1 (2)).

[4] See per Parke, B., Load v. Green, 15 M. & W. 216, 221, "as the goods were obtained by a fraudulent purchaser, the plaintiffs had a right to disaffirm it, and to revest the property in them." The vendor can retake them; In re Eastgate (1905), 1 K.B. 465.

[5] See Addie v. Western Bank, L.R. 1 H.L.Sc. 145, 165, per Lord Cranworth; Erlanger v. New Sombrero Co., 3 App. Cas. 1218, 1278 per Lord Blackburn.

the contract. Where the goods have come into the hands of a bona fide purchaser you cannot take them back[1]." The tendency of some of the American courts to base the rule on the principles of estoppel has resulted in decisions which require, in addition, that the goods must have been delivered by the original vendor to the fraudulent vendee before the re-sale. Thus, in *Barnard v. Campbell*[2], where the defendants purchased and paid for goods, which at the time were not in the vendor's possession but were subsequently obtained by fraud from the plaintiffs, it was held the plaintiffs could recover. The same principle would apply where the fraudulent vendee had obtained the possession before re-sale but without the knowledge and consent of the vendor[3].

The following rules relating to rescission, therefore, refer to bona fide purchasers whose purchase is subsequent to the alleged rescission.

The owner's right of rescission may be lost if in consequence of his delay the position even of the wrongdoer is affected[4]. Otherwise, he is only precluded from exercising his election by conduct amounting to a ratification, so that the title of the fraudulent vendee, no longer voidable, can be transferred to a sub-purchaser whether in good or bad faith. There can be no ratification without knowledge of one's rights and thus a sale induced by fraud is not affirmed by a judgment recovered in an action for the purchase money brought by the vendor in ignorance of the fraud[5]. Whilst mere lapse of time is no bar until there is something to raise suspicion[6], "it is a general principle of law founded both on justice and authority that even in cases of fraud, when a man has notice of any matter which gives him a right either to insist upon a contract or to treat it as void, he must say within a reasonable time whether he

[1] Per Blackburn, J., Lindsay *v.* Cundy, 1 Q.B.D. 348, 355.
[2] 55 N.Y. 456, 14 Am. Rep. 287; 58 N.Y. 73, 17 Am. Rep. 208.
[3] Dean *v.* Yates, 72 Ohio St. 388. Many cases under s. 23 of the Sale of Goods Act come under s. 25 (2), but as the principle there is that of the Factors' Acts delivery of possession is necessary.
[4] Clough *v.* L. & N. W. Rly. Co., L.R. 7 Ex. 26, 35, mere issue of a writ by a party privy to the fraud is not enough.
[5] H.L.R. VI. 311 quoting 25 N.Y. Supp. 200.
[6] Rawlins *v.* Wickham, 3 De G. & J. 304.

determines to go on or to avoid it[1]"; and this upon the ground that "lapse of time without rescinding will furnish evidence that he has determined to affirm the contract, and when the lapse of time is great, it probably would, in practice, be treated as conclusive evidence to shew that he has so determined[2]." Since the election once made is final and cannot be retracted a subsequent attempt at rescission before re-sale is unavailing[3].

An attempt at rescission would also be ineffective where the vendor refused to restore the purchase money or part of it already paid; indeed it seems he must on his own part offer to return it, unless the fraudulent party has rendered a return impossible or inequitable[4]. The commission of an act of bankruptcy by the vendee does not deprive the vendor of his right to rescind as it is well settled that the creditors only step into the bankrupt's shoes[5].

The action of tort being based on the rescission and therefore the non-existence of the contract, can be brought before the time limited for credit has elapsed, the vendee being deemed in tortious possession of the goods; but if the vendor affirms it he must affirm it in all respects and so cannot sue in contract before the credit has expired[6].

The mere fact that a person who obtains a voidable title may be criminally liable for the misdemeanour of obtaining goods by false pretences does not affect the vendor's position towards third persons (nor towards his vendee, for the rule as to prosecuting before bringing a civil action only applies to felonies)[7]. On the other hand, where the contract is void it

---

[1] Bramwell, B., in Morrison v. Universal Marine Insurance Co., L.R. 8 Ex. 40, 55.
[2] Clough v. L. & N. W. Rly. Co., L.R. 7 Ex. 26 at p. 34.
[3] Scarf v. Jardine, 7 App. Cas. 345, 360; Clough v. L. & N. W. Rly. Co. ubi sup., quoting Com. Dig. Election (2).
[4] Thurston v. Blanchard, 39 Mass. 18, 20; 33 Am. Dec. 700, per Shaw, C.J.; Phoenix Iron Works Co. v. McEvony, 47 Neb. 228.
[5] In re Eastgate (1905), 1 K.B. 456; the vendor may disaffirm even after the receiving order, Tilley v. Bowman (1910), 1 K.B. 745.
[6] Read v. Hutchinson, 3 Camp. 352; Ferguson v. Carrington, 9 B. & C. 59; Strutt v. Smith, 1 C. M. & R. 312.
[7] Parker v. Patrick, 5 T.R. 175, Sale of Goods Act, 1893, s. 24 (2). By the Indian Contract Act, s. 108, a person with a voidable title cannot transfer ownership if "the circumstances which render the contract voidable amounted to an offence committed by the person in possession or those whom he represents." In

is not necessary that the fraud should amount to larceny; although *Cundy v. Lindsay*[1] is difficult to distinguish from a case of larceny, for Blenkarn, though convicted of false pretences, was considered by the House of Lords not to have acquired even a "possessory title."

(iv) SALE IN FOREIGN COUNTRY.

The fact that goods sold in market overt in this country are the property of a foreigner domiciled abroad does not prevent the passing of the title. In the same way the sale of the goods of an Englishman domiciled here, giving a good title thereto according to the law of the country where the goods are situate at the time of the sale, is valid here also. Thus in *Cammell v. Sewell*[2] the master of a Prussian vessel sold the goods of an Englishman, which were on board his ship in Norway, in circumstances which gave the purchaser no title according to English law, but a good title according to the law of Norway, and it was held in the Court of Exchequer Chamber that such a sale deprived the owner of his title, on the principle that "if personal property is disposed of in a manner binding according to the law of the country where it is, that disposition is valid everywhere[3]." Thus, a sale in Germany by public auction in the recognized manner would confer upon the purchaser a good title to goods stolen in England[4].

(v) ALTERATION IN THE NATURE OF THE GOODS.

By the Roman Law a person who improperly obtained another's goods might acquire the ownership by his subsequent dealings with them—*e.g.* by using them to make a substance of a different kind (*specificatio*), or by attaching one thing to something else, so that it comes to be considered a mere part of the

some of these American states where false pretences amount to a felony the goods are recoverable even from an innocent sub-purchaser.
  [1] 3 App. Cas. 459; P. & W. on Possession, p. 108. Also G. W. R. Co. *v.* London County Bank (1901), A.C. 414.
  [2] 5 H. & N. 728.
  [3] Byles, J., dissented on the ground that a sale in market overt was not analogous, not being "at variance with any general law of nations," but the decision was approved in Castrique *v.* Imrie, L.R. 4 H.L. 414, 429, 438; Alcock *v.* Smith (1892), 1 Ch. 238, 268. See Dicey, *Conflict of Laws* (2nd ed.), 519.
  [4] German Civil Code, Arts. 935, 383.

other (*accessio*)—the former owner having an action for the value against the new one[1]. In the same way, the property might be altered by the acts of a purchaser from a wrongful taker. In a recent Scottish case[2] *A* purchased from *B* in good faith oil which *B* had no right to sell. With the oil and other materials he manufactured lard, which was sold to customers in the ordinary course of business. It was held that *A*, by creating a new species which could not be resolved into its original elements, became the proprietor of the substance manufactured, and was bound to pay a sum representing the value of the oil.

It is clear that in such a case both the taker and his vendee are in English law liable for conversion, for at least the original value of the goods. The question of the property in the resulting product is in our law subordinate to that of the right to the possession, which is now entirely within the discretion of the judge, who may hand the goods over to either party and order him to compensate the other[3]. The question of ownership has, however, been discussed in several cases though the principles of our law on the point are by no means settled.

Where the property of several persons is accidentally mixed together so as to become indistinguishable, a third person who takes it does not acquire ownership, as the owners become tenants in common[4]. It has been said that where the *confusio* or *commixtio* is brought about wilfully by one of the owners, he forfeits his own property to the other, but the matter is doubtful and, in any case, such a rule would not affect a bona fide purchaser from a wrongful taker[5].

It seems well established that the owner retains the ownership so long as he can identify the original materials, whatever alterations they may have undergone, *e.g.* where leather is made

[1] Inst. II. i. 25–34.

[2] International Banking Corpn. *v.* Ferguson, 1910, S.C. 182. It was admitted that the English rule was materially different. The question of ownership was important here, for as the defendant was not in possession, he would have been liable only for his profit, had he not become the owner.

[3] Salmond, *Torts* (4th ed.), p. 390.

[4] Jones *v.* Moore, 4 Y. &. C. Ex. 351; Buckley *v.* Gross, 3 B. & S. 566; Spencer *v.* Union Marine Insce. Co. L.R. 3 C.P. 427.

[5] Pop. 38; Ward *v.* Ayre, 2 Bulstr. 323, Cro. Jac. 366; Black. *Comm.* II. p. 405; Lupton *v.* White, 15 Ves. 432, 439; Salmond, *Torts* (4th ed.), 369 n (8); 2 Kent. *Comm.* (10th ed.), 466. In Colvill *v.* Reeves, 2 Camp. 575 it was held there can be no *commixtio* of articles of furniture.

into boots, or cloth into a coat, or trees squared into timber[1].
In New York it has even been held that wilful trespassers who
take corn and convert it into whisky acquire no title if the
owner can prove that his corn was used, but the question of
ownership did not directly arise and there was a strong dissenting opinion[2]. The property in chattels may also pass by
attaching them to the freehold. Thus, in the opinion of
Lindley, L.J.: " If I employ a builder to build me a house,
and he does so with bricks which are not his, I apprehend that
they become mine, and that their former owner cannot recover
them or their value from me," in accordance with the maxim
Quicquid plantatur solo, solo cedit[3].

The ownership of goods therefore passes either because
they become incapable of identification, or because they cease
to be goods; and, in either case, the good or bad faith of the
defendant would seem to be irrelevant to the question of ownership, though not to the more important one of damages.

(vi) PROPERTY PASSING BY SATISFIED JUDGMENT.

It is a good plea to an action by the owner against the
purchaser that the property has passed to the latter by satisfaction of a judgment for trespass, detinue or trover against the
wrongful obtainer.

It has been seen that a trespasser was formerly said to acquire the property in the goods taken, and after replevin became possible, the owner by bringing trespass was said to disaffirm the title[4]. The modern rule is that the property does
not pass till satisfaction of a judgment for the value of the
property. "*A* in trespass against *B* for taking a horse recovers
damages; by this recovery and execution done thereon the
property of the horse is vested in *B*. Solutio pretii emptionis
loco habetur[5]."

[1] Y.B. 5 H. VII. 15.
[2] Silsbury v. McCoon, 3 N.Y. (3 Comst.) 379, 53 Am. Dec. 307. "The
difficulty of proving the identity is not a good reason. It relates merely to the
convenience of the remedy, and not at all to the right." It was admitted that had
the change been made by the bona fide purchasers, the property would pass.
Bronson, C.J., took a different view as to trespassers also.
[3] Gough v. Wood, 1894, 1 Q.B. 713, 719.
[4] Ames, *Select Essays, etc.* III. p. 551.
[5] Jenk. Cent. (4th cent. 88), p. 187; cf. Keilw. 58b.

In the same way satisfaction of a judgment in trover or detinue against his vendor is a good plea by the purchaser. In *Adam v. Broughton*[1] it is said: "The property of the goods is entirely altered by the judgment obtained against *M*, and the damages recovered in the first action are the price thereof, so that now he hath the same property therein as the original plaintiff had; and this against all the world." In *Cooper v. Shepherd*[2], an action against a purchaser from a wrongful possessor of a bedstead, a plea was held good which amounted to this: "that *W* took and converted this bedstead, and, whilst he had it in his possession, the defendant bought it of him, and paid him for it, and that the plaintiff has recovered from *W* and has received from him the payment of damages for such conversion, being the full value of the bedstead[3]." Where the sale is before satisfaction the plea is based on the rule that the plaintiff is not entitled to damages beyond the value of the goods, where it is after the satisfaction it is like the plea of purchase in market overt: in the one case the property passes to the purchaser subsequently to the sale, in the other by the sale itself (but by a person who has become the owner).

In *Buckland v. Johnson*[4], Jervis, C.J., who was, however, dealing with the liability of joint tort-feasors, thought that the property passed by the judgment alone without satisfaction. But this dictum was overruled in *Brinsmead v. Harrison*[5], the decision in which was approved in *Ex parte Drake*[6] where Jessel, M.R., declared the theory of the judgment in an action of detinue to be that "it is a kind of involuntary sale of the plaintiff's goods to the defendant," an assessment of the value of the goods, which value the Court gives to the plaintiff as the next best thing to the goods themselves. If the plaintiff does not get that value, then the property in the goods remains in him. As "the chief business is the satisfaction," an accord with satisfaction has the same effect as a satisfied judgment, though "not so high" as a judgment[7]; and the damages must be estimated on the full value of the goods[8].

[1] Andr. 18; 2 Str. 1078.   [2] 3 C.B. 266.
[3] Per Tindal, C.J., p. 271.   [4] 15 C.B. 145, 162.
[5] 6 C.P. 584, 589.   [6] 5 Ch. D. 866, 871.
[7] Put v. Royston, 2 Show. 211, 213.   [8] Lacon v. Barnard, Cro. Car. 35.

The question might arise as to the time when the property passes. The satisfaction of the judgment might be held to relate back to the conversion, but there seems to be no decision on the point and it is stated that the doctrine of relation is contrary to the general principles of English law[1]. The practical working of the doctrine, where it holds good, is shewn by an American case[2], in which it was held that satisfaction of a judgment in trover for a female slave, related back to the conversion, so that two slave children, born in the interval, became the property of the defendant.

Where the wrongful vendor has consented to judgment for the value of the goods being entered up against him on the basis of a contract between him and the owner, no further action is possible against his purchaser even though the judgment by consent is unsatisfied and the vendor is adjudicated bankrupt, for the judgment, not being an ordinary judgment for the detention of goods, effects a legal transfer without satisfaction[3].

(vii) WAIVER OF TORT.

In the above-cited case[4] there was a transaction between the owner and the wrongful vendor which was affirmed as a contract by the form of judgment consented to; but even where there is no such contract the vendor may be sued for money had and received to the plaintiff's use. The contract upon which such an action is based being fictitious, it is no objection that such a vendor sold the goods, "as one that claimed a title and interest in them, and therefore could not be said to receive the money for the use of the plaintiff, which indeed he received to his own use[5]." Since the mere bringing of the action is the waiver of the tort and bars a subsequent action

---

[1] Chalmers, *Sale of Goods Act*, p. 11. Jervis, C. J. (15 C.B. p. 160), thought the property vested "by relation to the time of the conversion."
[2] White *v*. Martin, 1 Porter 215, 26 Am. Dec. 365.
[3] Bradley and Cohn *v*. Ramsay (1912), 106 L.T. 771. Before the rule was settled that satisfaction was necessary, it was said that the property only passed in detinue when the plaintiff by issuing process for the value renounced his right to the goods in specie. Note to 6 M. & G. 160 n (a). There can now be no renunciation till receipt of the money. In re Scarth, 10 Ch. 234; Mayne, *Damages* (8th ed.), p. 285.
[4] Bradley & Cohn *v*. Ramsay, *ubi sup*.
[5] Lamine *v*. Dorrell, 2 Ld. Raym. 1216; Moses *v*. Macferlan, 2 Burr. 1005, 1012.

against the purchaser, it is immaterial that the proceeds of
the goods are for some reason (such as bankruptcy) not received by the plaintiff[1].

The bringing of an action for money had and received is
not the only conclusive election to waive the tort. Thus, if the
owner treats the sale to the bona fide purchaser as valid for
the purpose of deriving an advantage in bankruptcy proceedings
against himself, this is a conclusive election[2]. The difficulty
arises in connection with ambiguous acts. The acceptance of
part of the proceeds does not amount to a waiver though it
would go in reduction of damages[3], but where there is a claim
for the proceeds amounting to a definite waiver of the conversion, the owner cannot, after part only of the proceeds is
paid, treat the seller or the purchaser as a wrongdoer. The
claim for payment for the goods may, however, only amount
to a "qualified offer to adopt the sale," i.e. if the defendant will
pay for the goods, so that on his refusal it is competent to the
plaintiff to repudiate the sale altogether[4]. Where the claim is
in the first place in trover and only alternatively for money
had and received, there is no waiver[5]; and where in the course
of the action an agreement is entered into by which a sum is to
be paid in full settlement of all claims against the wrongdoer,
without prejudice to the claim against the purchaser, there is
no bar to an action against the latter[6]. The mere application
of a judicial kind to the Court to obtain the proceeds of goods
improperly obtained is not conclusive proof of an election[7].

The principle of waiver is often said to be based on the
idea of a ratification, by the owner, of the contract between the
wrongful vendor and the purchaser[8]. It has also some likeness
to the doctrine of estoppel, based on the owner's election. "He
cannot say at one time that the transaction is valid, and thereby
obtain some advantage, to which he could only be entitled on

---

[1] Holt, C.J., in Lamine v. Dorrell, seems to have thought this doubtful.
[2] Roe v. Mutual Loan Fund, 19 Q.B.D. 347.
[3] Burn v. Morris, 5 Tyrw. 485.
[4] Valpy v. Sanders, 5 C.B. 886.
[5] Rice v. Reid (1900) 1 Q.B. 54; De Gorter v. Attenborough, 21 T.L.R. 19.
[6] Rice v. Reid, ubi sup.   [7] Morris v. Robinson, 3 B. & C. 196.
[8] But see Marsh v. Keating, 2 Cl. & F. 250, 1 Bing. N.C. 198; Hone v. Boyle,
27 L.R. Ir. 137.

the footing that it is valid, and at another time say it is void, for the purpose of securing some further advantage[1]." He cannot, in fact, blow hot and cold at the same time. That the effect of the owner's election, in giving the purchaser a good title, is only incidental, was clearly pointed out by Park, J., when delivering the opinion of the judges in the House of Lords in *Marsh v. Keating*[2], a case dealing with stock.

"Here the former owner of the stock does not seek to confirm the title of the transferee of the stock. No act done by her is done *eo intuitu*; it is perfectly indifferent to her, whether the right of the transferee to hold the stock is strengthened or not. She is looking only to the right of recovering the purchase money; and, if in seeking to recover that, she does not by her election make the right of the purchaser weaker, it can be no objection that she does not make it better. In fact, however, the interest of the purchaser...is so far collaterally and incidentally strengthened, that after recovering the price for which it was sold, she would effectually be stopped from seeking any remedy against, or questioning in any manner, the title of the purchaser of the stock[3]."

[1] Honeyman, J., Smith *v.* Baker, 8 C.P. 350, 357; Roe *v.* Mutual Loan Fund, 19 Q.B.D. 347.

[2] 2 Cl. & F. p. 286, 1 Bing N.C. p. 217.

[3] As seen above, there may be an election, though there is no recovery of the price.

CHAPTER V

LIABILITY WHERE THE PROPERTY HAS NOT PASSED

    (i) LIABILITY FOR CONVERSION
   (ii) RECOVERY OF THE GOODS IN SPECIE
  (iii) MEASURE OF DAMAGES
  (iv) RECAPTION
   (v) LOSS OF RIGHT OF ACTION

(i) LIABILITY FOR CONVERSION.

Though a purchaser who, by the mere purchase, becomes owner of the goods cannot be liable to an action for conversion, it has been suggested that he may sometimes be obliged to pay the price over again. *A* has been accustomed to deal with *B*, the agent of *C*, and to pay *C* by crossed cheque according to the trade custom. Finally, *B* obtains goods by fraud from *C* and sells them to *A*, who in good faith pays for them in cash at *B*'s request. Does *A*'s negligence make him liable to pay over again? It seems not; unless *A* has disobeyed explicit instructions to pay by crossed cheque[1].

A bona fide purchaser who does not acquire the ownership of the goods is usually liable in an action of conversion by the true owner. An action for the recovery of goods or their value lies (i) for wrongful taking, (ii) for wrongful detaining, (iii) for wrongful disposition. A purchaser from a wrongful taker was never liable in trespass for wrongful taking whether he acted in good or bad faith. " If a stranger takes my horse, and sells him, a trespass will not lie against the vendee, but a detinue[2]." The questions to be considered are therefore whether he is liable, (i) as a wrongful detainer, (ii) as a wrongful disposer of

---

[1] See International Sponge Importers Ltd. *v.* Watt (1911), S.C. (H.L.) 57 per Lord Loreburn, L.C. at p. 66.
[2] Day *v.* Austin, Owen 70,

another man's goods. Under the old forms of action detinue lay in the former case, in the second, trover and conversion; but the modern action of conversion now covers both, though in the first case it is still often called detinue. Since the Judicature Acts liability does not depend upon the form of action but upon the facts on which the plaintiff bases his claim, and actions for the recovery of goods are not framed precisely in detinue or conversion.

(i) It was long settled, under the old forms, that a refusal to deliver up the goods on demand was evidence of a conversion; and it has been strongly urged that, under the modern extensive conception of conversion, it is, in itself, a conversion in law[1]. However, when a jury returns a special verdict of demand and refusal it was said by Coke to be the judge's duty to enter judgment for the defendant.

In order to establish the defendant's liability both demand and refusal must be unqualified. Thus where the owner demanded that a gun, which had burst, whilst in the defendant's possession, should be restored to him in its original state, a refusal was held no evidence of a conversion[2].

If a person found in possession of another's goods were to surrender them at once to the first claimant, the presumption would be strong that he had not acquired them in good faith[3]. It is therefore just that he should be protected by a rule that refusal is not conversion unless unqualified. He is allowed time to make inquiries and to dissipate his natural doubts as to the title. Thus a refusal to deliver goods till the claimant proves that he is the real owner has been held no evidence of conversion[4]. But a refusal by a servant to deliver goods until the plaintiff had seen his master, who was not then to be found, was held evidence of conversion, in an action against the master[5]. Where the refusal is unqualified, and made under a claim of right an action lies though it be retracted or not persisted in, if the defendant who is in possession refuses to deliver, or to

[1] Salmond, *Torts*, s. 97. Cf. 10 Co. Rep. 56 b–57 a.
[2] Rushworth *v.* Taylor (1842), 3 Q.B. 699.
[3] See Dent *v.* Chiles, 5 St. & P. (Ala.); 26 Am. Dec. 350, commenting on Green *v.* Dunn (next note).
[4] Green *v.* Dunn, 3 Camp. 215.
[5] Pillot *v.* Wilkinson, 32 L.J. (N.S.) Ex. 201.

J.   6

allow the plaintiff to take the goods[1]. It was held in *Clayton v. Le Roy*[2] that, when the possessor becomes aware that the goods have been stolen, the mere communication to the owner of the fact that they have come into his possession, and a request to know his wishes in the matter, do not amount to evidence of an intention to detain wrongfully. Nor does a subsequent refusal to deliver them up to an agent who shews no evidence of authority. It is, in every case, a question of fact, whether the refusal means an intent to apply the goods to the defendant's use, or to keep them in order to ascertain the title to them and whether a reasonable time for doing so has not elapsed[3]. These rules apply equally to vendees[4] and pledgees[5] in good faith.

It is a good defence that the defendant is unable to comply with the demand owing to his being no longer in possession of the goods. Thus, in an action for trover of a deed, the evidence of a conversion was that, when the deed was demanded, the defendant said he would not deliver it, but that it was in the hands of his attorney, who had a lien upon it. Lord Ellenborough said: "The defendant would have been guilty of conversion if it had been in his power, but the intention is not enough. There must be an actual tort. To make a demand and refusal sufficient evidence of a conversion, the party when he refuses must have it in his power to deliver up or to detain the article demanded[6]." In another case, Parke, B., said there cannot be an effectual demand and refusal, "unless the party has at the time possession of the goods, and has the means of delivering them up[7]."

(ii) Where the facts do not amount to conversion by way of detention, there may be liability on the ground of disposition. For the method by which possession has been changed may

[1] Burroughes *v.* Bayne, 29 L.J. (N.S.) Ex. 185.
[2] (1911) 2 K.B. 1031. Scrutton, J., in the court below and Vaughan Williams, L.J., in C.A. thought there was a conversion.
[3] Vaughan *v.* Watt, 6 M. & W. 492, 497.
[4] Cooper *v.* Willomatt, 1 C.B. 672.
[5] Singer Manufacturing Co. *v.* Clark, 5 Ex. D. 37 where it was held that the Pawnbrokers' Act 1872 (s. 25) gave no protection against the true owner.
[6] Smith *v.* Young, 1 Camp. 439. This might have been treated as a wrongful disposition. See Hiort *v.* Bott, L.R. 9 Ex. 86, per Cleasby, B. at p. 92,
[7] Edwards *v.* Hooper, 11 M. & W. 363, 367.

be a conversion in itself so as to make a demand unnecessary. Mere removal of the goods, *e.g.* placing papers in the hands of the person's solicitor, is no conversion[1]. In *Hollins v. Fowler*[2] two tests were suggested. Blackburn, J., was of opinion that the only acts which do not amount to a conversion are those which would be consistent with the duty of a mere finder or bailee, such as safeguarding by warehousing or removal for that purpose. Brett, J., on the other hand, thought the question was whether "there was an intent to interfere in any manner with the title or ownership in the chattels, not merely with the possession." It was held by the House of Lords in accordance with the opinion of Blackburn, J., that any person who, however innocently, obtains possession of goods from a person who cannot give a good title to them, and disposes of them, whether for his own benefit or that of any other person, is guilty of a conversion. It is immaterial that the only profit he derived was a broker's commission. This rule would clearly cover a re-sale by a bona fide purchaser. It has been held, in an American case, that the refusal by innocent purchasers of stolen goods to pay the proceeds of the sale to their rightful owner was a conversion of the goods themselves[3].

Where a bona fide pledgee of tobacco had been repaid his advance, and had delivered up the possession to the pledgor before the true owner discovered his loss, it was held that no action lay. There was no wrongful detention, as the defendant had ceased to possess, and the re-delivery was not a wrongful disposal[4]. Bigham, J., likened the case to that of a carrier who conveys stolen goods and delivers them up to the thief at the end of the journey before the true owner demands possession[5]. On the other hand delivery to the pledgor after notice of a third person's title is clearly a conversion[6]. A bona fide purchaser does not escape liability by a re-sale to his vendor even before notice of the owner's title; he has the property in the goods, not merely a temporary possession like that of a pledgee or carrier, and a re-sale to his vendor is as inconsistent with

---

[1] Canot *v.* Hughes, 2 Bing. N.C. 448.   [2] L.R. 7 H.L. 757, 767.
[3] McDaniel *v.* Adams, 87 Tenn. 756.
[4] Union Credit Bank *v.* Mersey Docks & Harbour Board (1899), 2 Q.B. 205.
[5] At p. 216.   [6] Singer Manufacturing Co. *v.* Clark, 5 Ex. D. 37.

the true owner's title as a sale to any other party[1]. It is clearly
covered by the dictum of Lord Holt, in *Baldwin v. Cole*[2],
that the "very assuming to oneself the property and right of
disposing" of another's goods is a conversion. A sale after
notice of another's title is an obvious conversion.

Again, there is no liability in conversion when the defendant
has lost the goods through carelessness; his liability, if any,
results from the law of negligence not of conversion[3], and only
arises when he is under a duty to the plaintiff. Such a duty
can hardly arise when the purchase is in good faith, for there
cannot be a duty to a person of whose existence one is unaware[4].
In the absence of carelessness, *e.g.* where the goods have been
stolen without any fault of his, there is no liability of any kind[5].

A purchaser who is not liable for detention or disposal, can
only be sued in conversion if his purchase itself is a tortious
act. This question, one of more theoretical interest than practical importance, is most likely to arise in dealing with the
running of time under the Statutes of Limitation[6].

In *McCombie v. Davies*[7], an agent employed to purchase
tobacco for the plaintiff, bought it in his own name and pledged
it to the defendants, who were ignorant of the facts, by transferring it from his own name in the King's warehouse into
theirs. The defendants refused to restore it on demand. Lord
Ellenborough quoted the above-cited words of Lord Holt in
Baldwin v. Cole[8], and said : "Certainly a man is guilty of a
conversion who takes my property by assignment from another
who has no authority to dispose of it ; for what is that but
assisting that other in carrying his wrongful act into effect ?"
These words were only dicta, as there had been a demand and
refusal sufficient to establish liability, but in a later case, he
again said: "The very act of taking goods from one who has
no right to dispose of them is in itself a conversion[9]." In

---

[1] See Salmond, *Torts*, s. 105.　　[2] 6 Mod. 212.
[3] Williams *v.* Geese, 3 Bing. N.C. 849.
[4] Except, of course, where there is a duty to him as one of the public, an exception inapplicable here.
[5] Ross *v.* Johnson & Dowson, 5 Burr. 2825.
[6] Clayton *v.* Le Roy (1911), 2 K.B. 1031, per Fletcher Moulton, L.J. (p. 1048).
[7] (1805) 6 East 538, 540.　　[8] 6 Mod. 212.
[9] Hurst *v.* Gwennap, 2 Stark. N.P.C. 306, 307.

v]   LIABILITY IN OTHER CASES   85

Burroughs v. Bayne[1], Martin, B., said he was not inclined to
state "that the simple taking possession by the defendant
under the bill of sale was not a conversion of the goods"; and
in *Hilbery v. Hatton*[2] the same learned judge held that a person
who adopted a purchase by his agent of a ship wrongfully sold,
was guilty of conversion, though he had no knowledge of the
facts. In the former case, however, his remarks were not
necessary to the decision, and the decision in the latter can
be supported on other grounds for the defendant had instructed
the agent to make a hulk of the vessel. The dicta of Lord
Ellenborough were cited and approved by Fry, L.J., in *Fine
Art Society v. Union Bank of London*[3], and by Collins, M.R.,
in *Gordon v. L. C. & M. Bank*[4], cases where it was held that
the taking of a postal order or crossed cheque by a bank from
a person without any title to it, and receiving the money for the
wrongdoer, as in the first, or taking his indorsement as in the
second, gave rise to an action of conversion.

On the other hand there are two cases which seem directly
to the contrary. In *Spackman v. Foster*[5] title deeds of the
plaintiff were fraudulently taken from him in 1859, and without his knowledge deposited with the defendant, who took
them innocently to secure payment of a loan. The plaintiff,
on discovering his loss in 1882, demanded the deeds of the
defendant and, upon his refusal, brought an action to which
the defendant pleaded the Statute of Limitations. It was held
that, until demand and refusal, he had no right of action against
which the Statute would run. The decision was based by
Grove, J., on the ground that the defendant was like a depositee
or bailee until the demand and that there was no claim of title
to the deeds; the dicta of Lord Ellenborough were held
inapplicable to a defendant who only claimed the right of
safekeeping until repayment of the debt. The decision in
Miller v. Dell[6] was to the same effect and based upon very

[1] (1860) 29 L.J. (N.S.) Ex. 185, 189.   [2] (1864) 33 L.J. (N.S.) Ex. 190.
[3] (1886) 17 Q.B.D. 705, 712. The mere receipt of the order as the property of the
person handing it in was thought to be strong evidence of conversion, pp. 709, 711.
[4] (1902) 1 K.B. 242, 265 varied on another point in the House of Lords (1903)
A.C. 240.
[5] (1883) 11 Q.B.D. 99.
[6] (1891) 1 Q.B. 468; cf. Donald v. Suckling, L.R. 1 Q.B. 585 where a pledgee

similar facts. The result of these cases is that the taking of goods in pledge is not in itself a conversion.

In support of the rule that mere purchase is a conversion we have therefore only dicta, whilst the cases which seem to decide the contrary refer to pledgees, and are based on grounds that expressly exclude vendees.

The American cases on the subject may, consequently, be examined with advantage. The preponderating opinion is clearly in favour of the rule deduced from *McCombie v. Davies.* Thus, in *Hyde v. Noble*[1], it was definitely decided that " purchasing the property from one who had no right to sell, and holding it to their own use, is a direct act of conversion without any demand and refusal....It is only where the party obtains the possession lawfully, that it is necessary to shew a demand and refusal." Again, in a case in 1888 where the English cases were cited and discussed[2], it was clearly stated that " a possession taken under a purchase from one without title, and who has himself been guilty of a conversion in disposing of the goods or chattels, is a possession unauthorised and wrongful in its inception, and which the absence of evil intent in the purchaser cannot make rightful or lawful. Such a possession is based on the assumption of a right of property or a right of dominion over it, derived from the contract of sale, and what is this, in the legal sense, but a wrongful intermeddling or asportation or detention of the property of another[3]?"

So far we have dealt only with cases where the possession has been transferred in pursuance of the sale. Even in the American Courts it is held that the mere purchasing of property from one, who is neither the owner, nor authorised by him to sell is not sufficient to constitute a conversion, unless followed by the purchaser's taking actual or virtual

---

was held to have a special property, and Halliday *v.* Holgate, L.R. 3 Ex. 299 where Willes, J., thought a pledge intermediate between a lien and a mortgage.

[1] (1843) 13 N.H. 494, 499, 38 Am. Dec. 508, 513, per Parker, C.J.

[2] Velsian *v.* Lewis, 15 Or. 539, 543, 3 Am. St. Rep. 184, 188, per Lord, C.J. The principle was said to be inherent in the common law doctrine of *caveat emptor*, inapplicable here under the Sale of Goods Act.

[3] The doctrine that mere purchase and possession is no conversion is said to be found chiefly in cases where there was no improper obtaining by the vendor, *i.e.* where he has a limited interest.

possession[1]. It has also been held that, in order to dispense
with the actual taking of possession, any words relied on must
be unequivocal; they must "show defiance of the owner's
right—a determination to exercise dominion and control over
the property, and to exclude the owner from the exercise of
his rights[2]." But the decisions are not all in accord.

Such authority as exists in England is naturally against
liability where there is no possession. In *Mallalien v. Laugher*[3]
Best, C.J., stated that even if a purchase were tortious, possession
would be necessary. He thought that Lord Ellenborough in
McCombie v. Davies had gone to the extreme verge of the
law, but that the decision in that case could be supported, as
there had been a change in the state of the property by a
transfer in the dock-books "which, it is well known, is as much
a transfer for the purposes of trade, as an actual removal from
one warehouse to another." Indeed, it is well settled that even
a sale of another's goods is, in itself, no conversion unless possession is delivered in consequence of it[4]. " It is clear that there
can be no conversion by a mere bargain and sale without a
transfer of possession. The act, unless in market overt, is merely
void, and does not change the property or the possession[5]." If
this be so, it is obvious that the purchaser cannot be liable.

It seems clear that a demand would be necessary where
the purchase is in market overt and the property has revested
on conviction, for the acquisition of the goods was not unlawful.

A purchaser in good faith is not jointly liable with the
wrongful vendor in the absence of some subsequent joint conversion[6]. If a verdict be obtained against the vendor, who is
allowed by the bona fide purchaser, who has acquired the
property, to hand the thing back, and the vendor at the same

[1] Traylor v. Horrall, 4 Blackf. 317 where the English cases were discussed.
There was notice here, which makes the case stronger.
[2] Gillett v. Roberts, 57 N.Y. 28, 33. A demand was here held to be necessary.
[3] 3 C. & P. 551, 553.
[4] Lancashire Waggon Co. v. Fitzhugh, 6 H. & N. 502; Johnston v. Stear,
15 C.B. (N.S.) 330.
[5] Consolidated Co. v. Curtis (1892), 1 Q.B. 495, 498, per Collins, J.
[6] Nicoll v. Glennie, 1 Mau. & S. 588 ; Chamberlin v. Shaw, 18 Pick. (35 Mass.)
287, 29 Am. Dec. 526, per Shaw, C.J.; Larkins v. Eckwurzel, 42 Ala. 322, 94 Am.
Dec. 651.

time demand it back in the purchaser's name, the latter is not estopped from claiming its return[1].

According to the Roman Law an action for the goods could not be brought against a person who was not in actual possession, except (i) where the purchaser had parted with them in order to avoid liability (qui dolo desiit possidere), in accordance with the maxim *dolus pro possessione est*; or (ii) where he had defended the action as if still in possession (qui liti se obtulit), *e.g.* in order to give a third party time to acquire by usucaption[2]. The law of Scotland makes a purchaser out of possession liable, not only where he learns the facts before re-sale, but also where he innocently makes a profit by the re-sale (quantum lucratus)[3].

(ii) RECOVERY OF THE GOODS IN SPECIE.

When the defendant is still in possession the owner will probably wish to recover the goods in specie and on this point the difference formerly seen between the old forms of action in detinue, which was for the recovery of the goods themselves, and trover, which was for damages only, survives between conversion when based on detention and the same action when founded on a wrongful disposition. But since the owner may treat the refusal to restore the goods as evidence of wrongful disposal, he has now the option either of suing for damages for the value in the first instance, or only in default of recovery of the goods themselves. On the other hand, it was formerly equally within the option of the defendant whether he would give up the goods or pay damages for them, for as has been seen, since the decay of the appeal of larceny the common law has known no action ensuring the return of the goods in specie[4]. Thus in *Phillips v. Jones*[5] Parke, B., said: "Upon referring to the precedents it appears that the plaintiff in detinue has a right to recover the goods in specie, and in case of non-delivery, the value, and the option of giving up the goods or paying the value is in the defendant, who, by refusing to deliver the former renders himself liable to pay the latter." There was a corresponding

---

[1] Sandys v. Hodgson, 10 A. & E. 472.   [2] Girard, p. 340.
[3] Vallange v. Scot (1531), Mor. 10597; Scot v. Low (1704), Mor. 9123; Bell's *Principles*, 3, 527.
[4] Keilw. 64 b per Frowike, C.J. (20 H. 7).   [5] 15 Q.B. 859, 867.

difference in the forms of judgment entered in such case. In trover judgment was for the damages found by the jury; in detinue the defendant was ordered to restore the goods or in default their value, together, in either case, with damages for the detention[1]. Thus, in *Paler v. Hardyman*[2], it was held that judgment was wrongly entered for the goods *or* their value, and that it ought to give the option to the defendant and not to the plaintiff. Even in detinue, judgment was entered for the value in the first instance if it appeared that the goods were no longer in existence[3].

The usual claim now is for the recovery of the goods or their value together with damages for the detention, and the usual form of judgment is for a sum of money as damages in respect of the value of the goods and their detention, to be reduced to a smaller amount if the goods are returned to the plaintiff within a certain time. Moreover, though the plaintiff might not be able to obtain re-delivery of the goods, his right was always to the possession of them, the defendant having a power, not a right to refuse possession[4]. Of this privilege the defendant was deprived by the Common Law Procedure Act, 1854[5], which gave the Court, on the plaintiff's application, the power to order execution to issue for the chattel itself in any action for the detention of a chattel, without giving the defendant the option to retain the thing on the payment of the value assessed.

The defendant in an action for detention or conversion of goods can plead in mitigation of damages that the plaintiff accepted them after commencement of the suit[6], but the plaintiff can offer evidence as to their condition in order to determine the amount of the reduction[7]. The defendant may often wish to stay proceedings upon delivery of the goods to the plaintiff in the course of the action together with payment

---

[1] Rastall's Entries, tit. *Det.* Judgment, s. 7.
[2] Yelv. 71. Not " Quod quer recuperent dolium ferri vel valorem eiusdem " but " Quod recuperent dolium & si non valorem inde." Also Peters *v.* Hayward, Cro. Jac. 682.
[3] Viner, Abr. *Det.* E. 1 pl. 39 ; Bro. Abr. *Det.* pl. 25.
[4] Eberle Hotel Co. *v.* Jonas, 18 Q.B.D. 459 per Bowen, L.J., p. 468.
[5] 17 & 18 Vict. c. 125 s. 78 ; R.S.C. Order XLVIII.
[6] Moon *v.* Raphael, 2 Bing. N.C. 310.
[7] Williams *v.* Archer, 5 C.B. 318 ; McGrath *v.* Bourne, Ir. Rep. 10 C.L. 160.

of costs. On the ground that "an estimated value is a precarious measure of justice compared with the specific thing[1]," and that the modern action of conversion takes the place of the old action of detinue[2] this would usually appear just and reasonable. It seems, however, that whilst the action of detinue was in common use this was not allowed in trover except with the plaintiff's consent and, afterwards, the Courts urged as a reason against this course that the Court "did not keep a warehouse." But they ordered a stay where money was in question[3] and Lord Mansfield thought the above-mentioned ground a "false conceit" rather than an argument. Consequently, after the middle of the eighteenth century the principle was applied to articles which were not perishable or cumbrous[4]. Thus in trover for a packet of letters, the defendant was allowed to have proceedings stayed as to one of them, upon delivering it up and paying costs and damages[5]. If the plaintiff refuse such terms, he may proceed, but the Court will permit the defendant to deliver up the goods and the plaintiff must pay the costs of the action after such delivery in case he only obtains nominal damages for the goods in question[6]. But the rule does not apply where there are circumstances which may enhance the damages above the real value, or where there is uncertainty as to the quantity or quality of the thing[7], also where the plaintiff claims special damages or where the defendant merely offers to refer the assessment to an officer of the courts[8].

(iii) THE MEASURE OF DAMAGES.

The most important question in this connection is that of the measure of damages. As a purchaser cannot be a trespasser there is no place for punitive damages, and the principles on which the assessment is based are the same in all courts for all actions for the unlawful detention of another's

---

[1] Lord Mansfield, Fisher v. Prince, 3 Burr. 1363, 1365.
[2] Wilmot, J., ib.
[3] Pickering v. Truste (1796), 7 T.R. 53.
[4] Hart v. Skinner (1844), 16 Vt. 138; 42 Am. Dec. 500, where the history of the English rule was discussed. Cf. Makinson v. Rawlinson (1822), 9 Price 460, where it was held not to apply to a horse.
[5] Earle v. Holderness, 4 Bing. 462.
[6] Ib.; also Peacock v. Rhodes, 8 Dowl. 367.
[7] Fisher v. Prince, 3 Burr. 1363.
[8] Whitten v. Fuller, 2 W. Bl. 902 ; Tucker v. Wright, 3 Bing. 601.

property[1]. The defendant is liable for the value of the goods and for any loss caused by the detention. Any damage beyond the value must be specially claimed by the plaintiff and separately assessed by the jury. Where in trover for a horse it was laid as special damage that the plaintiff had been obliged to hire horses, damages were assessed at the value of the horse when taken, and the sum paid for hire, deducting what would have been the expense of keeping his own horse for the time[2]. There may be an act upon the defendant's part which brings loss on the plaintiff not amounting to the full value of the goods, *e.g.* where the defendant leaves the horse at an inn where the owner cannot recover it except on payment of charges[3], but the question most likely to arise relates to the assessment of the value of the goods. It is here that the position of a bona fide purchaser is to some extent different from that of other persons who handle goods which do not belong to them[4].

It was held in *Armory v. Delamirie*[5] that the value of a jewel not produced in court was to be estimated against a *spoliator* as that of a stone of the first quality. In *Mortimer v. Cradock*[6] a necklace of 56 brilliants, £500 in value, was missed by the plaintiff. The defendant, within three weeks of the loss, sold to different parties, diamonds, part of the necklace, and which were clearly identified, to the value of £190. The defendant gave an unsatisfactory account of the persons who sold them to him and did not produce them at the trial. It was held that the jury might fairly be directed to presume that the whole set came to the defendant's hands; and that the full value of the necklace was the proper measure of damages. But where the defendant is a bona fide purchaser the plaintiff must prove the value of each article lost and the defendant's liability in respect of each, for " when in such a case a defendant is put to pay over again, the plaintiff should be required to prove his case in the strictest manner[7]." In an

---

[1] Lord Halsbury, L.C., The " Mediana," 1900, A.C. 113, 118.
[2] Davis v. Oswell, 7 Car. & P. 804.
[3] Buller, J., Seyds v. Hay, 4 T.R. p. 264.
[4] See Mayne, *Damages* (8th ed.), pp. 453–484.   [5] 1 Str. 505.
[6] (1843) 12 L.J., C.P. 166.   [7] Haris v. Shaw, Cas. t. Hard. 349.

action of assumpsit for goods sold and delivered by a liquor
merchant, the only evidence was that of servants who were
altogether ignorant of the contents of the bottles delivered ;
Lord Ellenborough directed the jury to presume that the
bottles were filled with the cheapest liquor the plaintiff dealt
in, viz. porter[1]. However, it is not necessary to prove the
precise contents of boxes containing miscellaneous goods, *e.g.*
clothes ; and where the defendant, though a bona fide purchaser, suppresses the means of ascertaining the truth, the
presumption is in favour of the plaintiff[2].

The bona fide purchaser has also to be distinguished from
other defendants, in considering the time at which the value
of the goods is to be estimated.

When the market value of the property is fluctuating, this
may be one of three points,—the time (1) of the conversion,
(2) of the commencement of the action, (3) of its highest value
between these two points. Eminent judges have differed on the
question in England[3] and in America[4]. The English practice
seems to be to leave it to the jury as a matter of discretion[5],
but the Act of 1833 which allows the jury to give interest
over and above the value at the time of the conversion seems
impliedly to fix the latter as the proper moment at common
law[6]. In the United States the question has, it seems, always
been considered one of law[7].

The same difficulty arises when the nature of the goods
has undergone alteration, for the comparative unimportance
of the question of the ownership has thrown greater stress
upon the rules relating to the time when the value is to be
assessed. Where fixtures are severed from the freehold it is
well settled that only their value as chattels can be recovered,
though less than their value as fixtures[8], but as conversion
never lay for realty this throws little light upon the general
rule. Goods which have ceased to be part of the freehold may,

---

[1] Clunnes *v.* Pezzey, 1 Camp. 7.   [2] See Butler *v.* Basing, 2 C. & P. 613.
[3] Cf. Mercer *v.* Jones, 3 Camp. 477 and Greening *v.* Wilkinson, 1 C. & P. 625.
[4] Kent and Story seem to have differed, see note to 1 Cab. & E., p. 92.
[5] Johnson *v.* Hook, 1 Cab. & E., p. 89.
[6] 3 & 4 W. IV. c. 42 s. 29.   [7] Page *v.* Fowler, 39 Cal. 412.
[8] Clarke *v.* Holford, 2 C. & K. 540; McGregor *v.* High, 21 L.T. (N.S.), 803.
The surplus may be obtained by suing for the damage to the land.

however, be increased in value by acts done after the severance. Thus in the case of severance of coal from the mine,
Parke, B., held that damages against a defendant who was
not guilty of fraud should be estimated at the market value
of the coalfield as if it had been purchased; but where there
is fraud the value is to be estimated as at the pit's mouth[1].
A bona fide purchaser of coal wrongfully severed by another
would therefore not be liable for an increase in value due to
some act of his own, e.g. transporting it to market, and, it
seems, could also claim the cost of raising it to the surface[2].
If his vendor had severed in good faith the purchaser would
only be liable for the actual loss to the land.

This rule was adopted in the courts of equity, and also by
the House of Lords in a case where Lord Cairns, after pointing
out that the defendants had acted in good faith, said: " I do
not understand that there is any rule in this country or in
Scotland, that you have a right to follow the article which is
taken away, the coal which is severed from the inheritance,
into whatever place it may be carried or under whatever circumstances it may come to be disposed of, and to fasten upon
any increment of value which from exceptional circumstances
may be found to attach to that coal[3]." These words were
quoted with approval by Lord Macnaghten in a subsequent
case, as being probably equally applicable to trover and detinue
of goods, and not restricted to questions of coal trespass[4].

The same point arose in *Reid v. Fairbanks*[5], where a ship
in an unfinished state was completed by a bona fide purchaser
and sent to sea. It was held that the damages were its value
at the time of the conversion, to be estimated by taking the
value of the completed ship and deducting therefrom the
money which would have had to be spent by the builder in
order to complete her according to the contract.

Thus the logical consequences of the common law rule,
that a defendant had no lien for any outlay bona fide made

---

[1] Cf. Martin v. Porter, 5 M. & W. 351 and Wood v. Morewood, 3 Q.B. 440.
The measure of damages for negligent severance is doubtful.
[2] See Morgan v. Powell, 3 Q.B. 278.
[3] Livingstone v. Rawyards Coal Co., 5 App. Cas. 25, 32.
[4] Peruvian Guano Co. v. Dreyfus (1892), A.C. 166, 174, where the cases are discussed.   [5] 13 C.B. 692.

have been evaded, the Courts having allowed juries to take
into consideration, in mitigation of damages, the payments
the plaintiff would have had to make if the defendants had
not made them[1]. Lord Macnaghten considered the question
still open whether there was "any rule founded on principle
or authority, which compels the court to enforce against a
defendant who has acted honestly though mistakenly, extreme
legal rights at the instance of a plaintiff who seeks to avail
himself of the assistance of the court for the purpose of
obtaining an unjust and unfair advantage[2]." These cases shew
the considerations by which the Courts will be guided in the
exercise of their discretionary power to order the specific
restoration of the goods upon terms. The matter is to some
extent complicated by the doubtful question whether the purchase itself is a conversion.

The English cases therefore draw a distinction between
acts enhancing the value of the goods done by a dishonest or
fraudulent wrongdoer and those done in good faith. In one
American case it was decided that where the goods are in the
hands of a bona fide holder the owner cannot claim the value
of improvements effected by the wrongdoer. The defendants
innocently purchased cord-wood from thieves who had manufactured it out of timber cut from the plaintiff's land, and they
were held liable for its value at the time of the taking with
interest. "The original owner has the 'title' to this timber,
and as against the thief, the title to the results of the thief's
labour, the wrongdoer, as it were, being estopped from setting
up any claim by virtue of the wrong he has done. Against
the innocent purchaser from the thief, the original owner still
has the 'title' to his timber, but by virtue of what does he
now have title to the thief's labour? The estoppel, so to call
it, being created by fraud or wrong, exists only against the
one guilty of that fraud or wrong, which the purchaser is not,
and while it is effectual against the wrongdoer, the reason for

---

[1] Jervis, C.J. (13 C.B. p. 729) thought that, though in strictness the defendant
might have no right to deduct the cost of his outlay, no jury would give such
damages; "they would always give what they conceived the plaintiff justly entitled to."
[2] (1892) A.C. 174.

it does not exist as against the innocent man, as to whom it therefore fails[1]." In the earlier case of *Silsbury v. McCoon*[2] it was held, on the contrary, that the damages should be based on the right of recaption, and that if the innocent holder, believing himself to be the owner, converts the chattel into a thing of a different species, so that its identity is destroyed, the original owner can only recover its value at the time of the purchase[3]. Whatever may be the English doctrine as to recaption the decision in this case seems to be more reasonable and more in accord with the English rules relating to damages than that in the former case. Though the innocent purchaser ought not to suffer from his own acts done in good faith, there is no good ground for giving him the benefit of an enhanced value wrongfully created by his vendor and which the vendor himself could not have claimed.

It has been suggested as the true rule on the question of the property in the goods, that the ownership of the improvement never does, in fact, vest in the original owner; but that there is a distinction between the right of recaption and that to damages. Since his property in the subject matter continues, the owner has a right to have it back in value or in specie; in the latter case the improvements must follow because they cannot be separated; in the former they need not[4]. The English cases are not, however, based on the theoretical question of the property in the goods, and by leaving the question to the discretion of the jury the Courts have been able to avoid laying down any rigid rules.

A defendant who has distrained a horse damage feasant after it has ceased to do damage, cannot claim, in mitigation of damages the cost of feeding it, for he has held it of his own wrong[5]. On the other hand, it has been held that a bona fide purchaser who has bought stolen beasts in market

---

[1] Railway Co. *v.* Hutchins (1877), 31 Ohio St. 571 where the English cases were discussed.
[2] (1844) N.Y. (6 Hill) 425, 41 Am. Dec. 753. The decision in 4 Den. 332, which repudiated the view that the parties' rights depend upon motive, was reversed (1850), 3 N.Y. (3 Comst.) 379, 53 Am. Dec. 307.
[3] 3 N.Y. (3 Comst.) 386, 53 Am. Dec. 307 per Ruggles, J. See also Rockwell *v.* Saunders, 19 Barb. 473.
[4] Mayne on Damages, *loc. cit.*
[5] Wormer *v.* Biggs, 2 C. & K. 31.

overt cannot, in answer to a claim for them by the original owner in whom the property has revested on conviction, counterclaim for the cost of their keep, for they were his own property until conviction[1]. This would seem to imply that, where ownership is not acquired such a counterclaim by an innocent purchaser would be successful, but it would be an anomalous result that a purchase in market overt should be less favourably treated than a purchase elsewhere. Moreover expenses incurred in feeding animals are different from those which enhance the value of the property.

It has been held in the United States that the purchaser has no lien for the cost of repairs made to a chattel without the owner's consent[2]. In this connection it is interesting to note the Roman distinction between "necessary" expenses without which the property would have perished or deteriorated, and "useful" expenses which have actually improved its value[3]. A bona fide purchaser could keep the goods until his outlay on these two classes was reimbursed. A mala fide purchaser, whose act did not amount to *furtum*, could only claim his necessary expenses, but in Justinian's time was allowed to take away any improvements if this were possible without harm to the property[4].

The Roman Law contained elaborate rules relating to the fruits and produce of things held by a bona fide possessor. Though he became the absolute owner of them, those not yet consumed (*fructus exstantes*) had to be restored, *i.e.* his ownership was divested[5]. There is no corresponding rule in the common law[6], but the jury are expected to take into consideration the possibility of such fruits when assessing the value of the thing producing them.

[1] Walker *v.* Matthews, 8 Q.B.D. 109.
[2] Clarke *v.* Hale, 34 Conn. 398.
[3] Girard, p. 341 n (3), D. 50. 16. 79. It seems that repairs were impensae "necessariae" not "utiles," the latter not including expenses "quae deteriorem esse non sinant."
[4] D. 6. 1. 38, 48; C. 3. 32. 5.
[5] Girard, p. 321. The wool of sheep or young of cattle would be classed as *fructus.*
[6] "The rule of the civil law, happily the rule in Scotland, though most unfortunately never introduced into our jurisprudence." Lord Brougham, Aberdeen Rly. Co. *v.* Blakie, 1 Macq. p. 479.

(iv) RECAPTION.

Though the question of ownership can be evaded in the discussion of damages, it must be faced when dealing with the right of recaption. Most of the cases in the Year Books on the rule of market overt are based on a recaption of the goods by the original owner, so that the action of trespass, in the law of personal, as of real property, has been largely used to decide questions of title. In fact, the right of recaption was generally recognized as the test of ownership[1], but being a measure of self-help was jealously regarded by the courts. In the time of Britton it was only allowed *flagrante delicto, i.e.* on the day of the taking and on fresh pursuit ; otherwise, the owner lost his goods "because our will is that everyone proceed rather by course of law than by force[2]." After the decay of the appeal of larceny these restrictions as to time were relaxed, but other limitations were gradually imposed.

An owner cannot enter upon land, or break into a house, in order to seize goods, simply because they are his own[3], but he can do so where they have been taken by the wrongdoer upon his own land, for they came there by his own wrong[4]. It has been held that the same rule applies to an innocent person's land where the goods have been put there with his assent[5]. This probably should be understood to mean that the occupier must have known of the wrongful act and not merely of the placing of the goods on his land, but it was stated generally by the Court that "when the defendant's beasts are taken from him by wrong, and are not out of his possession by his own delivery, he may justify the taking of them in any place he finds them." In a slightly later case, however, it was said that the owner can only enter a third party's land when the goods have been feloniously taken[6], and, again, that the third party's assent to, or knowledge of the placing of the goods on his land does not give the owner the

---

[1] Y.B. 6 H. VII. 7 pl. 4, Keble *arg.*   [2] Britton I. 57, 116.
[3] Taylor *v.* Fisher, Cro. Eliz 246; Anthony *v.* Haney, 8 Bing. 186. See In re Eastgate (1905), 1 K.B. 465 as to right to break into house of wrongful taker.
[4] Y.B. 9 Ed. IV. 35 per Littleton, J., quoted Rolle, Abr. *Trespass*, 9; Patrick *v.* Colerick, 3 M. & W. 483.
[5] Chapman *v.* Thumblethorp, Cro. Eliz. 329.
[6] Higgins *v.* Andrews, 2 Rolle 55.

right to enter to seize them where there has been no felony[1].
Such is the rule laid down by Blackstone[2]: "If, for instance,
my horse is taken away, and I find him in a common, a fair
or public inn, I may lawfully seize him to my own use; but
I cannot justify breaking open a private stable or entering
on the grounds of a third person, to take him except he be
feloniously stolen, but must have recourse to an action at law."
Thus where there is no felony the prohibition against entry
on an innocent third person's land seems absolute; but
Tindal, C.J., thought that if there was a refusal to deliver up
the property or to answer the owner's demand, "a jury might
presume a conversion, or at any rate the owner might, in such
a case, enter and take his property subject to the payment of
any damage he might commit[3]."

Where there is no question of entry upon land it is un-
doubted law that the owner can peaceably retake the goods[4].
Whether he can use force is more doubtful. We have seen
that formerly, this was only possible where the taking and
retaking were almost one act, but the well-known case of
Blades v. Higgs[5] decided that, according to the present law,
the owner may forcibly retake his goods even from a bona
fide purchaser, provided a demand is first made and refused.
The cases cited in argument for the right to retake were either
cases of retaking from a wrongdoer, or of defence of possession
against a person endeavouring to disturb it; against it, were
cited cases of entry upon land. It was admitted by the Court
that there was no direct authority either way and the decision
was based on two grounds:

(i) It is clear that possession may be defended against a
wrongdoer, and "if the defendants were the owners of the
chattels, and entitled to the possession of them, and the

---

[1] Masters and Poolie's case, 2 Rolle 208.
[2] *Comm.* III. p. 4.
[3] Anthony *v.* Haney, 8 Bing. p. 187. Cf. 47 Am. Dec. 267 where no request is
said to be necessary.
[4] Ex p. Drake (1877), 5 Ch. D. 866, 871, where Jessel, M.R., said: "Under the
circumstances we must consider it established that the property remained in the
plaintiff. That being so, he had a right to obtain possession of his property by
taking it peaceably or by means of proper legal process."
[5] (1861) 10 C.B. (N.S.) 713, 719.

plaintiff wrongfully detained them from him, the defendants in law would have the possession, and the plaintiff's wrongful detention against the request of the defendants would be the same violation of the right of property as the taking of the chattels out of the actual possession of the owner."

(ii) The Court followed the decision in *Harvey v. Brydges*[1], which dealt with forcible re-entry on land, and the reasoning of Parke, B., who said : " I cannot see how it is possible to doubt that it is a perfectly good justification to say that the plaintiff was in possession of the land against the will of the defendant, who was owner, and that he entered upon it accordingly; even though in so doing a breach of the peace was committed[2]."

Even if mere purchase is a conversion, a demand is essential upon the first ground; but the decision is contrary to the law laid down by Britton and is considered doubtful by learned writers[3]. The analogy of fresh pursuit or self-defence is not convincing; and though Blackstone allows entry on a bona fide purchaser's land when the goods are stolen, he is careful to add: "So it be not in a riotous manner, or attended with a breach of the peace[4]." If the case is to be defended it must be on other considerations of policy[5]. Again, in the case of land the Statutes of Forcible Re-Entry give a security which is not present here. At any rate, it is clear that no more violence may be used than is necessary to retake the goods; and the case does not warrant an imprisonment or detention for an indefinite time[6]. Hale[7] says that an owner of goods may justify beating a trespasser, but if death follows it is manslaughter. Therefore an innocent purchaser cannot be wounded or maimed even after a refusal to deliver, but *Blades v. Higgs* is important because a right to commit a battery may reduce a homicide to manslaughter[8]. If the possessor himself use force it is in

---

[1] 14 M. & W. 437.

[2] See, *contra*, the American cases, Barnes *v*. Martin, 15 Wis. 240, 82 Am. Dec. 670; André *v*. Johnson, 6 Blackf. 375.

[3] P. & M. II. p. 167; Pollock, *Torts* (10th ed.), p. 406.

[4] *Comm.* III. p. 3. See 47 Am. Dec. 267; the riot or excessive force would not give the detainer the right to recover it from the owner.

[5] Holmes, J., in Commonwealth *v*. Donahue (1889), 148 Mass. 529, 12 Am. St. Rep. 591.   [6] Harvey *v*. Mayne, Ir.R. 6 C.L. 417.

[7] P.C. I, p. 485.   [8] See note to 3 Fost. & F. 205 (b).

defence of an illegal possession and, therefore, an assault; and "if death ensues as the consequence of a wrongful act, which the party who commits it can neither justify nor excuse, it is not accidental death but manslaughter[1]."

(v) LOSS OF RIGHT OF ACTION.

That the right of recaption depends upon ownership and not upon the right to bring an action, is shewn by the fact that it can exist where the taker cannot bring an action. His right of action may be lost in two ways (i) by lapse of time, (ii) by judgment against one of two wrongdoers.

(i) The effect of lapse of time on the right to recover goods depends upon the statute 21 Jac. I. c. 16 which, though it barred the remedy, did not affect the right[2]. "It is pretty safe to assume that when the law may deprive a man of all the benefits of what was once his, it may deprive him of the technical title as well[3]." However, this is not the law of England for the right of recaption survives the expiration of the six years limited by statute[4]; but this is probably true only of peaceable recaption, though the question is unsettled[5]. If the use of force be justifiable only after demand and refusal, the destruction of the right to make such a demand by lapse of time must also put an end to the right to retake the goods by force[6]. It has been suggested by Sir F. Pollock that the following views might be taken. "It might be held that possession so taken was so wrongful as not to be capable of coalescing with the true title. On the other hand it might be held that the force was a personal wrong for which an action might be brought, but that this made no difference to the character of the possession once acquired, and did not prevent the combination of it with the right to possess—a right not extinguished though not enforceable by action[7]."

"A conversion which has once taken place cannot be cured"

---

[1] Fenton's Case, 1 Lewin C.C. 179 per Tindal, C.J.
[2] See 1 Macq. p. 321 per Lord St Leonards.
[3] Holmes, J., Davis v. Mills (1903), 194 U.S. 451, 457.
[4] See however per Fletcher Moulton, L.J., Clayton v. Le Roy (1911), 2 K.B. p. 1048.
[5] Ex p. Drake (1877), 5 Ch. D. p. 871.
[6] Pollock and Wright on Possession, p. 114.   [7] Ib.

and therefore the action is barred when six years have elapsed from the time of the tortious act. Subsequent circumstances make no difference[1]. " It is a general rule that, when there has once been a complete cause of action arising out of contract or tort, the statute begins to run, and that subsequent circumstances which would but for the prior wrongful act or default have constituted a cause of action are disregarded[2]." As the vendor who has improperly obtained the goods is usually liable in tort, it has been argued on the authority of *Wilkinson v. Verity* that the action was barred six years after the first conversion not only against the vendor but against the vendee. But this view was emphatically repudiated in *Miller v. Dell*[3], the above-cited case being held applicable " only to an action against the defendant in respect of a wrongful act done by the defendant himself." The result is that as against the purchaser the time under the Statute begins to run from his conversion, though the original taking may have taken place more than six years before, and, as we have seen, the English Courts, at any rate in the case of a pledge, have held a demand and refusal necessary to establish a conversion. In *Spackman v. Foster*[4] the deeds were in the defendant's possession for 23 years before demand and refusal and yet it was held that the plaintiff's remedy by action was not barred. Time only begins to run when the refusal is a conversion, *i.e.* it must be unequivocal. " In order to make the title perfect, there must have been something in the nature of an adverse possession for more than six years[5]."

In those jurisdictions where merely taking possession under a purchase is held a conversion it might be argued, under the rule of fraudulent concealment, that time does not begin to run in favour of a bona fide purchaser till the owner knows of the sale to him. It is probable, however, that though this rule would apply to a thief or trespasser, who carried a stolen watch about in his pocket as watches are generally carried, it would not affect a bona fide purchaser who did so, for he cannot be

[1] Note (a) to 2 Wms. Saund. 47. Rolle, Abr. 5 (L) pl. 1.
[2] Wilkinson v. Verity, L.R. 6 C.P. per Willes, J., at p. 209.
[3] (1891) 1 Q.B. 468.   [4] (1883) 11 Q.B.D. 99.
[5] Plant v. Cotterill, 5 H. & N. 430, 439; Philpott v. Kelley, 3 A. & E. 106.

said to be fraudulent in any sense of that widely-extended term[1].

So far it has been presumed that the original taker parted with the goods before the action was barred against him. "What if *A* takes the goods of *B*, keeps them for six years and then sells or bails them to *C*? Can *B* demand them from *C*, and sue in trover on a refusal to restore them? The point seems never to have been decided, but it is submitted as clear on principle that no such action will lie. The original wrong-doer has acquired a right to retain possession of the property as against the true owner, and this right should be assignable and transmissible. The owner, indeed, still retains a nominal ownership, but he has no longer the *jus possidendi*, which is now vested in the wrongdoer and in those who claim under him[2]."

(ii) A judgment against the wrongful taker of goods may be a bar to a subsequent action against a bona fide purchaser provided that the property in the goods has been transferred by satisfaction[3]. Thus an unsatisfied judgment against a master of a ship for selling the goods he has agreed to transport is no bar to an action of trover against his vendees for conversion[4]. Satisfaction of a judgment for trespass against a wrongful taker is also no bar, where the recovery was for the taking only and not for the value of the goods[5]; so where judgment for 40s. was entered in an action for trespass of two horses this was held no bar "for 40s. cannot well be imagined to be the value of the horses[6]." On the other hand it has been seen that the owner may affirm the property to be in the wrongful vendor though there is no satisfaction[7].

A bona fide purchaser is not a joint wrongdoer with the taker as a result of the sale alone but may become such on a subsequent act of conversion. He may also, of course, be a joint purchaser. In this case judgment against one is a good

[1] See per Field, J., in Chapin *v.* Freeland, 56 Am. Rep. 701.
[2] Salmond, *Torts*, p. 361.
[3] Broome *v.* Wooton, Yelv. 67. See above, p. 75.
[4] Morris *v.* Robinson, 3 B. & C. 196, Hyde *v.* Noble, 38 Am. Dec. 508.
[5] Lacon *v.* Barnard, Cro. Car. 35.
[6] Field *v.* Jellicus, 3 Lev. 124.
[7] Bradley *v.* Ramsay (1912), 106 L.T. 77.

defence in an action against the other, though unsatisfied[1]. It seems, however, that subsequent detention and refusal to deliver by the other is a new conversion for which a second action can be brought[2]; the result being as if the first conversion were committed by a different party. In this way the English Courts indirectly arrive at the same conclusion as the American Courts, which hold that an unsatisfied judgment is no bar against a joint converter.

Even when a judgment against a joint wrongdoer is a good defence the right of recaption still exists for there is no change in the property. So independent of the remedy by action is the right of recaption, that it is laid down by Littleton that a release of all personal actions does not destroy it[3]; and in *Put v. Rawsterne* it was held to survive a judgment for the defendant in trespass[4]. This could only be so where the taking and not the property was the subject of the judgment and the same principle would apply where the defendant succeeded in trover on a purely technical ground, *e.g.* that the refusal was not unequivocal[5]. The jury in estimating damages against a bona fide purchaser cannot take into consideration that a right of action also exists against the wrongful taker[6].

[1] Buckland *v.* Johnson, 15 C.B. 145; Brinsmead *v.* Harrison, 6 C.P. 584.
[2] Brinsmead *v.* Harrison, *ubi sup.* It would seem (on the reasoning in Wilkinson *v.* Verity) that this would only be so where the first demand had been made to the defendant alone.
[3] Ten. ss. 497, 498.
[4] 2 Mod. 319; Skin 57. See Ames, *Select Essays*, etc. III. p. 571.
[5] *E.g.* as in Clayton *v.* Le Roy (1911), 2 K.B. 1031.
[6] The dicta to the contrary in Morris *v.* Robinson, 3 B. & C. 196 are severely criticized in Mayne on Damages (8th ed.), p. 135.

CHAPTER VI

RESTITUTION

THE rule that, where the owner's statement of claim discloses a felony for which the defendant should have been prosecuted, the plaintiff is not allowed to make the felony the foundation of a civil action until the "dignity of the law is vindicated" by a prosecution[1], does not prevent an action for conversion against a bona fide purchaser from the felon even before the latter's prosecution[2]. The purchaser's position is, however, often affected by the fact that his vendor has been guilty of felony in obtaining the goods.

In the twelfth and thirteenth centuries, the *actio furti* though a criminal proceeding, could by the omission of the "words of felony" be used as a civil action against an innocent purchaser from the thief, and was a means of recovering the goods themselves. As criminal and civil remedies became more distinct, its place was taken by the appeal of larceny, a purely criminal prosecution in which more attention was given to the possessor's intent, and by various civil remedies which did not secure the return of the goods in specie[3]. The value of the appeal lay in the fact that on the felon's conviction the owner could recover his goods from third persons by a "writ of restitution[4]"; but as many stringent conditions, such as fresh suit, had to be fulfilled[5], and as the writ became more and more to be regarded as a favour in the discretion of the King's officers, this mode of procedure gradually fell into disuse. In

---

[1] The latest English case is Smith v. Selwyn (1914), 3 K.B. 98; see also Carlisle v. Orr (No. 2), 1918, 2 I.R. 442.

[2] Stone v. Marsh, 6 B. & C. 551; Marsh v. Keating, 2 Cl. & F. 250, 1 Bing. N.C. 198; White v. Spettigue, 13 M. & W. 603, where it was suggested that such an action might not be maintainable against a mala fide purchaser.

[3] P. & M. II. pp. 152–168; Holdsworth, H.E.L. III. p. 271.

[4] For an example see Rastall's Entries, *Appeal*, Restitution 25, also Golightly, v. Reynolds, Lofft p. 91.

[5] Ames, *Select Essays*, etc. III. 420, 421; Markham v. Cobb, W. Jones, 147; as to fresh suit, Stamford, P.C., III. c. 10, f. 165.

fact, after the rise of the prosecution by way of indictment, it often happened that the owner came on the scene to find that the felon had already been convicted, and that the goods in the latter's possession had been forfeited to the King in the same way as those of which he was owner[1]. It seems to have been customary at one time to stay proceedings on indictment for a year, in order to allow appeals to be brought, but as the evidence for the Crown often perished as a result, this was eventually abandoned[2]. In order to prevent injustice to the owner, the statute 21 H. VIII. c. 11 was passed. This statute provided that if the thief were indicted and found guilty, or otherwise attainted, by reason of the evidence of the owner or of any other by his procurement, the owner should be "restored" to his property; and that the justices before whom the thief was tried, should have power under the Act to award, from time to time, writs of restitution as if the felon "were attainted at the suit of the party in appeal."

The effect of the statute is to give the diligent owner the same privileges as on a conviction by way of appeal, whilst exempting him from the necessity of making fresh suit. As Hale says: "It is regularly true, that of what things the owner shall have restitution upon the Statute 21 H. VIII. he should have restitution upon a conviction in an appeal at common law and è converso, so that what is said upon that statute is applicable to restitution upon appeal[3]." Thus the position of a bona fide purchaser under the statute is the same as it formerly was on a conviction by appeal, and it is clear that it is only when there has been a sale in market overt or some similar disposition that difficulty arises, for other purchasers have no more claim than the thief. The question was not likely to arise before the statute, for though such a sale would most probably be in market overt, yet where the sale was by the felon there was probably no fresh suit, and

[1] Thus the thief was said to have the property, see P. & M. II. p. 166; cf. Dalton, *Sheriffs*, p. 81 "a felon hath no property in goods stolen, but the property doth always remain in the right owner, which property in this case he also forfeiteth or loseth to the King, for default of pursuing the thief."
[2] Markham *v.* Cobb, W. Jones, 147, 148.
[3] P.C. I. 538.

where it was by the King's officers, as was usually the case[1], the possibility of a conviction in an appeal, was, as has been seen, very remote. When the question arose after the statute, the judges therefore had first to decide a somewhat academic point.

In the absence of authority, opinion seems at first to have been divided. Thus, in *Markham v. Cobb*[2] in 1626 the judges seem to have thought that no writ would have been awarded before the statute against a purchaser in market overt and, therefore, none would issue under the statute. The case of Market Overt is inconclusive on this point as it was decided that there was no sale in market overt. Coke[3], on the other hand, is clearly of the opinion that the appellor could have the writ " because of the fresh and diligent suit and pursuit of record; the goods were so protected thereby, and by the King's seizure, that the property of the same being *tanquam in custodia legis*, cannot be altered by sale in market overt." In this view he is supported by Hale[4], who, after exhaustively discussing the subject, concludes that there is no authority to the contrary, whilst reason and justice are in its favour.

The opinion of the judges at the time of the passing of the statute is said to have been, that it did not affect purchases in market overt[5]. But in spite of this and whatever may have been the law before the statute in the case of appeals, it seems that the judges at the beginning of the reign of Charles I, soon after the decision in *Markham v. Cobb*, resolved that the owner should have restitution from such a purchaser. As a result a practice of granting restitution grew up at the Old Bailey which became so well-established as to prevail even with judges who thought it should never have been introduced[6]; and this is the rule now laid down by the Sale of Goods Act, 1893, s. 24 (1). " Where goods have been stolen and the offender is prosecuted to conviction, the property in the goods so stolen

---

[1] Both Coke, 2 Inst. p. 714, and Blackstone, *Comm.* II. p. 450, imply that the King's officers were the usual sellers of stolen goods, and that the statute was passed to prevent such sales. [2] W. Jones, 147.
[3] 2 Inst. p. 714, this reasoning would not apply where the sale was not by the King's officers.
[4] P.C. I. p. 538 *sq.*; Hawkins, P.C., c. 23 s. 54.
[5] Per Williams, J., Chichester *v.* Hill (1883), 52 L.J., Q.B. 160, 164.
[6] See Kelyng, 35, 47 ; Kelyng changed his opinion as a result of the practice. Hale, P.C. I. 542, 544.

revests in the person who was the owner of the goods, or his personal representative, notwithstanding any intermediate dealing with them, whether by sale in market overt or otherwise[1]."

The wording of this section settles a question which might have arisen both under the Statute of 1529, where the words used are "the owner shall be restored" to his property, and under the later statutes[2] which provide that "the property shall be restored to the owner," namely:—what is the purchaser's position between sale and conviction? In *Horwood v. Smith*[3] the purchaser in market overt resold the goods before conviction in spite of notice of the theft which had meanwhile been given him. Though it was held that he was not liable in trover, the property during the interval was thought by Lord Kenyon to have remained *in dubio*, Lord Denman in *Peer v. Humphrey*[4] thought the expression hasty and was of opinion that "a sale in market overt clearly gives a *prima facie* title to the purchaser"; and in *Scattergood v. Sylvester*[5] it was decided that the full ownership was in the purchaser until revested by the conviction, a view confirmed by the Sale of Goods Act.

Another, more important, question arose in *Nickling v. Heaps*[6] for it was there held that the conviction not only revested the property, but related back to the offence, so that the prosecutor was not liable for taking back the goods from a bona fide purchaser before the conviction, which subsequently followed, on the ground that the goods were his own all the time, by relation. This view is clearly contrary to the decision in *Horwood v. Smith*, and the Court of Queen's Bench in *Lindsay v. Cundy*[7] was strongly of opinion that "restored" meant "restored from the time of conviction." This view is supported by the decision that a purchaser cannot counterclaim for the expenses of feeding stolen cattle, seeing that until conviction they were his own[8].

---

[1] In *Reg. v. Horan*, I.R. 6 C.L. 293 the property was held to revest after two sales in market overt. This section does not expressly say that the owner must prosecute. See 42 & 43 Vict. c. 22 s. 7 as to prosecutions by the Director of Public Prosecutions.

[2] 7 & 8 Geo. IV. c. 29 s. 57; 24 & 25 Vict. c. 96 s. 100; 6 & 7 Geo. V. c. 50 s. 45 (1).

[3] 2 T.R. 750, 755.   [4] 2 A. & E. 495, 498.   [5] 15 Q.B. 506.

[6] 21 L.T.N.S. 754.   [7] 1 Q.B.D. 348, overruled on other grounds.

[8] *Walker v. Matthews*, 8 Q.B.D. 109.

The Statute of 1529 related to stolen goods only, and it was consequently held in *Parker v. Patrick*[1] that if goods be obtained from *A* by fraud not amounting to larceny and pawned to *B* without notice, and *A* prosecute the offender to conviction and get possession of the goods, *B* may maintain trover for them. The case was said to be distinguishable from that of felony; "for there by a positive statute the owner, in case he prosecute the offenders to conviction, is entitled to restitution: but that does not extend to this case, where the goods were obtained by the defendant by a fraud." The subsequent statutes[2] though, like that of 1529, they did not mention third parties, provided for restitution in cases of convictions for misdemeanour as well as felony; and, after doubts had been thrown on *Parker v. Patrick*[3], it was decided, though reluctantly, in *Bentley v. Vilmont*[4] that the acts made no difference between convictions for false pretences and theft as regards the position of third parties. In this case, the sale, itself sufficient to give a good title, had taken place in market overt so that it had a double claim to validity; and the decision overruled the earlier case of *Moyce v. Newington*[5] where Cockburn, C.J., held that the statutes did not apply to purchasers from a vendor with a voidable title. The expressions of the House of Lords in *Bentley v. Vilmont* led to the re-establishment of the rule of *Moyce v. Newington* by the Sale of Goods Act[6] which enacts that "where goods have been obtained by fraud or other wrongful means not amounting to larceny, the property in such goods shall not revest in the owner by *reason only of the conviction of the offender*." These somewhat ambiguous words do not prevent the revesting of the property where, though the prisoner has been convicted on a charge of false pretences, the evidence shews that the offence of larceny has really been committed[7]; nor where the property has, be-

---

[1] 5 T.R. 175; R. *v.* De Veaux, 2 Leach C.C. 585.
[2] 7 & 8 Geo. IV. c. 29 s. 57; 24 & 25 Vict. c. 96 s. 100.
[3] See Peer *v.* Humphrey, 2 A. & E. 495, 498, per Lord Denman.
[4] 12 App. Cas. 478; also Nickling *v.* Heaps, 21 L.T., N.S. 754; Lindsay *v.* Cundy, 1 Q.B.D. 248, esp. Blackburn, J.'s judgment.
[5] 4 Q.B.D. 32.
[6] S. 24 (2); also 6 & 7 Geo. V. c. 50, s. 45 which applies only to "goods" within the meaning of the Sale of Goods Act.
[7] R. *v.* Walker (1901), 65 J.P. 729.

fore the re-sale, been revested in the owner by the disaffirmance of the prisoner's voidable title; for the act does not take away his common law rights[1]. The property also revests when the prisoner has pleaded guilty to an indictment of larceny in addition to one of false pretences[2].

The result seems to be that, although s. 24 (1) of the Sale of Goods Act provides that the property in the stolen goods is revested on conviction, the question whether the offence really amounts to larceny may be re-opened in a civil court, the conviction being a *res inter alios acta*[3].

The method provided by the Statute of 1529 for the recovery of the goods was by the award of writs of restitution in the same manner as though the felon had been attainted in an appeal. These writs were always very rare. Not only did Alderson, B., say in 1850[4] that in his experience he never knew an instance, but Lord Mansfield, in 1771[5], said they had not been awarded for two hundred years. The restitution, which is said to have become common at the Old Bailey in the early part of the seventeenth century, must, therefore, have been by way of a summary order of the Court, and since 1827[6] the Court has had statutory power to award the writ or to make a summary order. The latter is, obviously, in most cases more convenient from the owner's point of view, but there is no doubt that the Court can award the writ instead. Thus, in *Reg. v. Macklin* an application was made by an innocent pledgee for the issue of a writ in place of the usual summary order, and such a request will be granted when the Court is satisfied that the civil rights of the parties should be inquired into.

The statutes in giving a particular remedy do not take away those which the owner already has, so that the criminal remedies do not exclude the ordinary remedy by civil action[7]. Nor is the order or writ a condition precedent to the revesting

---

[1] R. v. George, *ibid.*   [2] R. v. Bianci (1903), 67 J.P. 443.
[3] Justice v. Gosling, 12 C.B. 39; Petrie v. Nuttall, 11 Ex. 569.
[4] Reg. v. Macklin, 5 Cox. C.C. 216. The only instance he could find was Burgess v. Coney, 1 Trem. P.C. 315 " which although a civil case, was tried here at the Old Bailey."
[5] Golightly v. Reynolds, Lofft 88.   [6] 7 & 8 Geo. IV. c. 29, s. 57.
[7] Golightly v. Reynolds, Lofft 88.

of the property, but "cumulative to the ordinary remedy by action," and "more in the nature of execution than anything else[1]."

The result is that the civil rights of the owner and purchaser may come before Criminal Courts acting under statutes based upon the maxim " Spoliatus debet ante omnia restitui," and, on the other hand, difficult questions of criminal law may have to be settled by judges sitting in Civil Courts[2]. The position of third parties is rendered more doubtful by legislation like the Factors' Acts, by the principle of estoppel, and by the difficulty of distinguishing larceny by a trick from obtaining goods by false pretences. The precise effect of the orders consequent upon convictions on the rights of third persons may therefore lead to troublesome questions. Perhaps a distinction should be made between two sets of cases.

(i) The owner brings an action of conversion against the purchaser and fails, the Court holding that the goods were obtained by a fraud not amounting to larceny; subsequently he successfully prosecutes the vendor for larceny. Can the Criminal Court order the restitution of the goods to which the purchaser has already established his title in another Court? It seems that the Court ought to do so because the rights of the parties depend upon a question of criminal law, which is not, except incidentally, a matter for a Civil Court.

(ii) Where the purchaser bases his title on the Factors' Acts the Criminal Courts have recently tended to adopt a different policy. In *Reg. v. Wollez*[3], the purchaser had established a title under the Factors' Acts upon an action of conversion brought against him by the former owner, but it was held that the property revested on conviction and the Court ordered the restoration of the goods. It was thought that the Court had no choice but to make the order, and that a sale under the Factors' Acts could not give a better title than one

---

[1] Scattergood *v.* Sylvester, 15 Q.B. 506, 511, 512 ; Re Vautin (1899), 2 Q.B. 549.

[2] *E.g.* Whitehorn Bros. *v.* Davison (1911), 1 K.B. 463 where the difference between false pretences and larceny by a trick was discussed. Difficulties may also arise when the seller has found the goods.

[3] 8 Cox. C.C. 337.

in market overt. But in the later case of *Payne v. Wilson*[1], an order was refused against a purchaser from a person convicted of larceny as a bailee, in order that an action of conversion, which proved to be unsuccessful, might be brought.

The usual course at present is said to be to refuse an order in circumstances which raise difficult questions as to the civil rights of the parties, and to leave them to their remedies in the Civil Courts; and it has more lately even been said that "none of the Acts dealing with the restitution of stolen property were intended by the Legislature to alter the civil rights of the parties as they existed[2]." We have seen that a defence under the Factors' Act is not likely to be successful when the vendor has been guilty of larceny by a trick. On the other hand, the reasons adopted in *Payne v. Wilson* are applicable to defences founded on the principle of estoppel, for this principle where it applies to "improper obtaining," would be unaffected by the conviction of the vendor, unless, as seems clear, the words "or otherwise" in sect. 24 (1) of the Sale of Goods Act, cover the case.

Again, although the Court on a conviction for false pretences may order restitution on the ground that the offence was in fact larceny, it may often refuse to do so in order that the innocent purchaser should be given an opportunity to cross-examine the witnesses in another Court. Nor will the Court usually issue an order if the purchaser has not been called as a witness; and an opportunity will generally be given him to appear by counsel to shew cause why the order should not be made[3].

The order, when made, is strictly limited to the property produced and identified at the trial, and does not apply to all the goods mentioned in the indictment[4]. Where a person had been convicted of stealing a large quantity of articles, which were sold at a public auction to many persons, and only three of the articles were produced and identified at the trial, an appli-

[1] (1895) 1 Q.B. 653 the case was overruled on the question of title under the Factors' Act by Helby v. Matthews (1895), A.C. 471 but the other point remains unsettled.
[2] Leicester v. Cherryman (1907), 2 K.B. 101, 102, per Ridley, J.; see Attenborough, *Recovery of Goods*, p. 72.
[3] Reg. v. Ford (1869), 11 Cox. C.C. 320; Reg. v. Stancliffe (1869), ib. 318.
[4] Reg. v. Goldsmith (1873), 12 Cox. C.C. 594.

cation for an order against the other purchasers was refused[1]. These safeguards are obviously still more necessary when the prisoner pleads guilty and is convicted on his own confession. The method of enforcing the order is by writ of attachment[2]. Before 1907 there was no appeal from the order, since it was held to be an order "in a criminal cause or matter," but now the Court of Criminal Appeal can review any order for the restitution of property[3].

In accordance with the usage in appeals and with the practice at the Old Bailey, it was held that the Statute of 1529 authorised the restitution of the proceeds of the sale of stolen goods[4]. According to Hale[5]: "If A be robbed of an ox by B who sells him to C who keeps the money in his hands, and after kills the ox, and sells the flesh—or if the money be seized in the hands of the thief, A may, if he pleases, have a writ of restitution for the money"; but it has been decided more recently that an application for restitution of the proceeds ought only to be granted when they are in the hands of the criminal or an agent who holds them for him[6]. Moreover, as there cannot be restitution of both the goods and the proceeds, the purchaser can keep the goods in peace, when an application is granted for restitution of the proceeds in the hands of the criminal[7]. When an innocent purchaser, whether in market overt or not has to restore the property, the Court may, on his application, order the sum paid by him to be refunded out of any moneys which may have been taken from the prisoner on his apprehension[8,9].

---

[1] Reg. v. Smith (1873), ib. 597.   [2] Reg. v. Wollez, ubi sup.
[3] Reg. v. Justices of C.C. Court (1887), 18 Q.B.D. 314; 7 Ed. VII. c. 23, s. 6 (2). The order may be cancelled or varied though the conviction is not quashed.
[4] Haris' Case, Noy. 128; Hanberrie's Case cited in Hicks v. Holiday, Cro. Eliz. 661. The statute 21 H. VIII. c. 11 provides for the restitution of stolen money. See Bro. Abr. Prop. 34, as to appeals.   [5] P.C. I. 542.
[6] Reg. v. Justices C.C., 17 Q.B.D. 598 affd. 18 Q.B.D. 314; R. v. Powell, 7 C. & P. 640.
[7] R. v. London County Justices (1908), 72 J.P. 513.
[8] 6 & 7 Geo. V. c. 50, s. 45 (2).
[9] Where the goods are under £15 in value an innocent purchaser may be ordered by a Metropolitan magistrate to deliver them to the owner. Such an order does not prevent the purchaser bringing a subsequent action to recover possession. 2 & 3 Vict. c. 71, s. 40; Dover v. Child (1876), 1 Ex. D. 172. See also as to property pawned with pawnbroker, 2 & 3 Vict. c. 71, s. 27, 28; 35 & 36 Vict. c. 93, s. 30.

PART III

POSITION OF A PURCHASER, WHO ACQUIRES NO TITLE, TOWARDS

(I) The Vendor

(II) Third Parties

CHAPTER VII

POSITION OF PURCHASER TOWARDS

(i) VENDOR

(ii) THIRD PARTIES

THE purchaser's position towards sub-purchasers can be conveniently treated in connection with his relation to his vendor in so far as this relation depends upon contract.

(i) POSITION TO VENDOR.

By the Roman Law the sale of another's goods was perfectly valid as a contract, but the seller, though not bound to transfer the ownership of the thing, was under an obligation to give free and quiet possession[1]. A bona fide purchaser from a mala fide seller, *e.g.* from one who had improperly obtained the goods, was, by the only real exception to the rule, allowed to sue his vendor before eviction[2].

The rights of the purchaser under the common law have given rise to much discussion. Where there was an express warranty there was no doubt that the seller was liable and Lord Holt thought that where the seller was in possession the mere affirming the thing to be his own amounted to an express warranty[3]. Buller, J., later went further, saying: "If an affirmation at the time of sale be a warranty, I cannot feel a distinction between the vendor's being in or out of possession: and if there be any difference, it seems to me that the case is strongest

---

[1] Dig. 18. 1. 28 (Ulp.), rem alienam distrahere quem posse nulla dubitatio est : nam emptio et venditio est : sed res emptori auferri potest.

[2] *E.g.* he might have wished to manumit a slave ; Girard, p. 549 n. (3) ; Dig. 19. 1. 30 (1). The Roman rule has been superseded in France by Art. 1599 of the Civil Code which makes the sale voidable by the purchaser.

[3] Medina *v.* Stoughton (1700), 1 Salk. 210.

against the vendor when he is out of possession, because the vendee has nothing but the warranty to rely on[1]."

Where there was no affirmation, it was formerly said that the maxim *caveat emptor* applied, the English law recognizing no warranty of title[2]. Blackstone's statement[3] that a purchaser of goods "may have a satisfaction from the seller, if he sells them as his own, and the title proves deficient without any express warranty for that purpose," leaves open the question whether a seller by the mere act of sale sells "as his own," so as to raise an implied warranty. In *Morley v. Attenborough*[4], Parke, B., relying on the earlier statements of the rule thought they were strong to shew "that there is no such warranty implied by the law from the mere sale.... The question in each case, where there is no warranty in expressed terms, will be, whether there are such circumstances as will be equivalent to such warranty." The decision was to the effect that there is no implied warranty on a sale by a pawnbroker, but the circumstances above-mentioned are so common that the Court did not doubt that if articles are bought in a shop professedly carried on for the sale of goods, "the shop-keeper must be considered as warranting that those who purchase will have a good title." This led Lord Campbell to observe in *Sims v. Marryat*[5] that if Parke, B., was right, the rule is beset with so many exceptions that they well-nigh eat it up. In the case of *Chapman v. Speller*[6] the Court held that no warranty was implied in a sale by a sheriff of goods seized under a *fi. fa.*, but wished to guard against being supposed to doubt the right to recover back money paid upon an ordinary purchase of a chattel, where the purchaser does not have that for which he paid.

In *Eichholz v. Bannister*[7], where the goods were sold innocently in a job-warehouse, it was held that there is an implied

---

[1] Pasley *v.* Freeman (1789), 3 T.R. p. 58.
[2] Noy's *Maxims*, 42; Co. Lit. 102 (a), Bagueley *v.* Hawley, L.R. 2, C.P. 625, Bovill, C.J. p. 628, "I consider the general rule to be, that, upon the sale of goods, there is no warranty of title implied by law."
[3] *Comm.* II. 452, citing Furniss *v.* Leicester, Cro. Jac. 474, where there was an affirmation.
[4] (1849) 3 Ex. 500, 511-513.
[5] 17 Q.B. 281, 291.   [6] (1850) 14 Q.B. 621.
[7] (1864) 17 C.B. (N.S.) 708, 721, 724.

warranty in the case of goods sold in a shop or warehouse. The question was fully discussed and the Court came to the conclusion that the alleged rule *caveat emptor* was based on dicta only and was unsupported by justice and sound sense. The true rule was said by Erle, C.J., to be that "if the vendor by words or conduct gives the purchaser to understand that he is owner, that tacit representation forms part of the contract," whilst Byles, J., remarked that there could seldom be a sale from which these circumstances are absent.

Thus, whereas the rule in *Morley v. Attenborough* was, that there is no implied warranty unless there are such circumstances as will be equivalent to a warranty, the rule which resulted from *Eichholz v. Bannister* was, that "a sale of personal chattels implies an affirmation by the vendor that the chattel is his and therefore he warrants the title unless it be shewn by the facts and circumstances of the sale that the vendor did not intend to assert ownership, but only to transfer such interest as he might have in the chattel itself[1]." This rule is codified in the Sale of Goods Act, 1893 (s. 12), which enacts that there is an implied condition of title "unless the circumstances of the contract are such as to shew a different intention," and it is in harmony with the definition of a contract of sale in s. 1 (1) as one "whereby the seller transfers or agrees to transfer the property" in the goods to the buyer. The condition, being a term going to the root of the contract, enables the purchaser to rescind the bargain even before eviction ; but it does not prevent him from bringing an action for damage sustained. There are also implied warranties of quiet possession and freedom from encumbrances, enabling the purchaser to sue for damages[2]. The implied conditions of title seem to render of little value to an evicted purchaser the implied warranty of quiet possession, but the latter may perhaps be useful, in some cases, to a sub-purchaser from the bona fide purchaser himself. Thus a bona fide purchaser in market overt, who sells, is not liable under

---

[1] Benjamin on Sale (2nd ed.), p. 523 ; thus a sale by one who knows he has no title is a false pretence, Reg. v. Sampson (1885), 52 L.T.N.S. 772 ; also Edwards v. Pearson, 6 T.L.R. 220.

[2] S. 12 (2) and (3); for a definition of warranty, see s. 62. See also Benjamin on Sale (5th ed.), p. 673 ; Attenborough, *Recovery of Goods*, pp. 22, 185.

the implied condition on the revesting of the property, for he was the owner at the time of the sale ; but he might be liable under the implied warranty of quiet possession unless, as in the case of leases of land, it applies, in spite of the wide terms of the section, only to acts of the seller or those claiming under him.

It was formerly said that the sale of another's goods not only gave the purchaser no right of action, but did not prevent the vendor from suing for the price even after the eviction[1]. But it has been held that payment to the rightful owner is a good defence to such an action[2], if made before action brought or plea pleaded[3]. But under the Sale of Goods Act the implied condition would now enable him to rescind the contract, on receiving the notice, and to return the goods to the owner, though a refusal to hand them over to the latter, until a reasonable case had been made out, would be no conversion. When the owner brings an action against the purchaser the latter's right to recover the price he has paid is not a right of indemnity and the vendor cannot be brought in as a third party to the action[4].

In *Eichholz v. Bannister* the action was brought for the return of the price as on a failure of consideration. The question arises as to the measure of damages on a breach of the implied condition. It is well established that on a sale of realty, where the purchase money has not been paid and the vendor is ignorant of his own want of title, the purchaser can only recover the expense of investigating the title. The difference between realty and personalty in this respect was put thus by Lord Hatherley in *Bain v. Fothergill*[5]: "A contract for the sale of real estate is very different indeed from a contract for the sale of a chattel, where the vendor must have known what his right to the chattel is[6]. And further, in the case of chattels, we

---

[1] Noy's *Maxims*, c. 42, "If I take the horse of another man and sell him, and the owner take him again, I may have an action of debt for the money"; see Benjamin on Sale, p. 604.
[2] Dickenson *v.* Naul (1833), 4 B. & Ad. 638.
[3] Allen *v.* Hopkins (1844), 13 M. & W. 94.
[4] Marten *v.* Whale (1917), 1 K.B. 544.
[5] (1874) L.R. 7 H.L. 158, 210.
[6] This is not so where the vendor is a bona fide purchaser.

well know, as regards the larger part of those contracts at least, that the chattels are purchased with a view to resale, and there-fore the whole transaction between the parties is on the footing and the faith, that all the expense or loss that may be incurred, whether it be by the vendee being put to the expense of making an inquiry upon the subject, or whether it be by a loss of profit which he might have obtained if the chattel had been delivered to him, is within the contemplation of the parties, and that it is, therefore, assumed to be the actual contract which the vendor wished to enter into." Thus, on the latter ground, when the price has been paid the damages are not necessarily limited to this sum[1].

The rules as to implied conditions and warranties are more important for the purpose of ascertaining the position of the purchaser to sub-purchasers than his rights against the person who has improperly obtained the goods, for, as was said in *Morley v. Attenborough*, "if the vendor knew that he had no title, and concealed that fact, he was always held responsible to the purchaser as for a fraud." It is clear that the purchaser is not liable to a sub-purchaser for fraud, but it must be remembered that at one time the action on a warranty was an action in tort in the nature of deceit. Thus, in *Williamson v. Allison*[2] Lord Ellenborough, C.J., said: "If the warranty be the material averment, it is sufficient to prove that broken to esta-blish the deceit....No other proof was required...than the warranty itself and the breach of it." The practice of declaring in assumpsit on the warranty was said by him to have become common about 1750. Where the action was brought for deceit, in the absence of a warranty, it was, however, long settled that knowledge of want of title was necessary. Thus, in *Sprig-well v. Allen*, in 1649, an action failed against a vendor who had bought a horse at Smithfield, but had not had it legally tolled, as the plaintiff could not prove that the defendant knew

---

[1] The usual, but not universal, rule in America allows the price and interest. See note to Ann. Cas. 1912, B. 1340; Hoffman *v.* Chamberlain, 53 Am. Rep. 788 (40 N.J. Eq. 663).
[2] (1802) 2 East 446, 451. See Dale's Case, Cro. Eliz. 44, an action of deceit. Held knowledge must be alleged, "but if he had affirmed they were his own goods, then the action would lie."

it to be the horse of A.B. for "the scienter or fraud is the gist of the action, where there is no warranty[1]."

Since it is now settled that the sale itself, except in a few cases, amounts to a representation, it is only necessary to prove the vendor's knowledge of his want of title for "knowledge of the falsehood of the thing asserted is fraud and deceit[2]." In *Dale's Case*[3] it was held that an allegation of knowledge was necessary, but where the vendor has improperly obtained the goods the words of Anderson, J., the dissenting judge, that "it shall be intended that he that sold had knowledge whether they were his goods or not" would apply. This presumption could be rebutted in an action by the sub-purchaser against his vendor by proof of purchase by the latter in the usual course of business.

(ii) POSITION TOWARDS THIRD PERSONS.

When a bona fide purchaser acquires the title he can, of course, transfer it to sub-purchasers, even if they have notice. This rule has been long established in equity in the case of trusts, and the reasons there given apply to personal chattels to an equal, if not a higher degree[4]. The purchaser who does not acquire ownership has nevertheless a possessory title, sufficient under the rule in *Armory v. Delamirie*[5] to enable him to sue any person except the owner or anyone acting by his authority, "for against a wrong-doer possession is a title[6]." But he may have had his possessory title lawfully divested and so be unable to sue.

In *Buckley v. Gross*[7], B bought goods from one who had improperly obtained them and he was charged before a magis-

---

[1] Aleyn, 91 (23 C.I.); Derry v. Peek (1889), L.R. 14 App. Cas. 337.
[2] Buller, J., Pasley v. Freeman, 3 T.R. p. 58.
[3] Cro. Eliz. 44.
[4] Lowther v. Charlton (1741), 2 Atk. 242, "otherwise it would very much clog the sale of estates"; Mertens v. Joliffe (1756), Amb. 313, "to prevent a stagnation of property."
[5] 1 Str. 505; Bro. Abr. *Tresp.* 433, "si A prist lavers de W. sans cause, il ne list a J.N. de eux prender de luy, car il ad title vs. touts nisi vers le verie owner."
[6] Jeffries v. G. W. R. Co. 5 E. & B. 802, 805. The full value may be recovered, The Winkfield (1902) P. 42. Cf. D. 47. 2. 75 (Javolenus). Furtivam ancillam bona fide emptam cum possiderem, subripuit mihi Atticus, cum quo et ego et dominus furti agamus;...emptori duplo quanti eius interest aestimari debet, domino autem duplo quanti ea mulier fuerit.
[7] (1862) 3 B. & S. 566.

trate with the possession of goods supposed to have been stolen or unlawfully obtained but the charge was dismissed. The magistrate ordered the property to be detained under the Metropolitan Police Act and it was sold before the time, prescribed by the Act, had elapsed. It was held that *B* could not sue *C*, a purchaser from the police. Cockburn, C.J., said: "The plaintiff who had nothing but mere naked possession (which would have been sufficient against a wrong-doer) had it taken out of him by virtue of this enactment. As against the plaintiff, therefore, the defendant derives title, not from a wrong-doer, but from a person selling under authority of the justice, whether rightly or wrongly is of no consequence." The plaintiff "had no title beyond what mere possession gave, and so soon as the goods were taken from him by force of law, there was a breach in the chain of that possession." Blackburn, J., said: "Their (*i.e.* the police) possession was the possession of the true owner and not of the wrong-doer, whose possession was terminated by their taking possession." In a later case[1], where, upon the hearing by a magistrate of an application for extradition of a fugitive criminal on a charge of theft, certain articles were produced under a *subpoena duces tecum* by a witness who had purchased them from the accused in England, it was held that the purchaser's possessory title had been lawfully divested by reason of their passing out of his possession under the *subpoena*. The purchaser's possessory title may also be divested in the same way, when the police take possession of the goods for the purpose of the prosecution under a warrant for the arrest of the person charged with the theft[2].

[1] Reg. *v.* Lushington (1894), 1 Q.B. 420.
[2] Tyler *v.* L. & S. W. R. Co., 1 Cab. & E. 285.

INDEX OF CASES

Crook *v.* Jadis 16, 17
Crown Jewels Case, The 37, 40, 43
Cundy *v.* Lindsay 3, 4, 62, 64, 66, 73
Currie *v.* Misa 25, 26, 27

Dale's Case 119
Davis *v.* Jones 12
— *v.* Mills 100
— *v.* Oswell 91
Dawson *v.* Prince 20
Day *v.* Austin 80
— *v.* Savadge 43
Dean *v.* Yates 71
De Bussche *v.* Alt 53, 61
De Gorter *v.* Attenborough 61, 78
Delaney *v.* Wallis 38, 46
Dent *v.* Chiles 81
Derry *v.* Peck 54, 120
Devas *v.* Venables 23
Devoe *v.* Brandt, 25
Dickenson *v.* Naul 118
Dickinson *v.* Valpy, 53
Dixon *v.* Bovill 12
Donald *v.* Suckling 85
Doswell *v.* Buchanan's Exors. 29
Dover *v.* Child 112
Down *v.* Halling 29
Downshire (Marquis of) *v.* O'Brien 37
Drake, Ex p. 76, 98, 100
Draycot *v.* Piot 9
Dresser *v.* Norwood 19
Duff *v.* Budd 67
Dunstable's (Prior of) Case 39
Durrell *v.* Haley 69
Dyer *v.* Pearson, 16

Earle *v.* Holderness 90
Eastgate, In re 25, 67, 70, 72, 97
Easton *v.* Worthington 49
Eberle Hotel Co. *v.* Jonas 89
Edmunds *v.* Merchants' Despatch Transport Co. 66
Edwards *v.* Hooper 82
— *v.* Pearson 117
Egan *v.* Threlfall 15
Eichholz *v.* Bannister 116, 117, 118
Emanuel *v.* Dane 68
Erlanger *v.* New Sombrero Co. 70

Farquharson Bros. *v.* King 6, 56, 57
Farr *v.* Sims 25
Farrant *v.* Thompson 25, 33
Fearon *v.* Mitchell 42
Fenn *v.* Bittleston 7
Fenton's Case 100
Ferguson *v.* Carrington 68, 72
Field *v.* Jellicus 102
Fine Art Soc. *v.* Union Bank of London 85
Fisher *v.* Prince 90

Flad Oyen, The 33
Ford *v.* Hopkins 9
— *v.* Stuart 25
Foster *v.* Green 10
— *v.* Pearson 16
Foxcroft *v.* Satterthwaite 24
Freeman *v.* Cooke 53, 54, 56
— *v.* East India Co. 46
Fry *v.* Smellie 50, 54
Fuentes *v.* Montis 1, 55, 64
Furniss *v.* Leicester 116

Gamage, Ltd. *v.* Charlesworth's Trustee 68
Ganley *v.* Ledwidge 38, 46
Garrard *v.* Haddon 49
Gibb's Case 46
Giblin *v.* McMullen 18
Gill *v.* Cubitt 15, 16, 17
Gillett *v.* Roberts 87
Gladstone *v.* Hadwen 62
Glegg *v.* Bromley 26
Glubb, In re 65
Golightly *v.* Reynolds 109
Goodman *v.* Harvey 16, 18
Gordon *v.* L. C. & M. Bank 85
Gough *v.* Wood 75
Grant *v.* Vaughan 15
Graves *v.* Key 51
Green *v.* Dunn 81
Greening *v.* Wilkinson 92
Gregg *v.* Wells 52, 53
G.W. Rly. Co. *v.* London & County Bank 73

Hall *v.* Dean 9
Hallett's Estate, In re 10
Halliday *v.* Holgate 85
Hanberrie's Case 112
Hardman *v.* Booth 66
Hare *v.* Saloon Omnibus Co. 23
Hargreave *v.* Spink 42, 43, 45
Haris' Case 30, 112
— *v.* Shaw 30, 39, 91
Harrison *v.* Clark 61
Hart *v.* Moulton 68
— *v.* Skinner 90
Hartop *v* Hoare 43
Harvey *v.* Bridges 99
— *v.* Facey 15, 19
— *v.* Mayne 99
Heane *v.* Rogers 51
Heath *v.* Crealock 8
Helby *v.* Matthews 111
Hewitt *v.* Loosemore 18
Hiern *v.* Mill 20
Higgins *v.* Andrews 97
— *v.* Burton 65
Higgs (or Hicks) *v.* Holiday 9, 112
Hilbery *v.* Hatton 85
Hill *v.* Smith 44

GENERAL INDEX

For EU product safety concerns, contact us at Calle de José Abascal, 56–1°,
28003 Madrid, Spain or eugpsr@cambridge.org.